HIGH-PERFORMANCE
IGNITION
Systems

Todd Ryden

CarTech®

CarTech®

CarTech®, Inc.
39966 Grand Avenue
North Branch, MN 55056
Phone: 651-277-1200 or 800-551-4754
Fax: 651-277-1203
www.cartechbooks.com

Edit by Bob Wilson
Layout by Monica Seiberlich

ISBN 978-1-61325-080-8
Item No. SA79

Library of Congress Cataloging-in-Publication Data Available

Printed in China
10 9 8 7 6 5 4 3 2 1

Title Page: Moving the distributor (when it holds the trigger device) can control the ignition's trigger. However, there is much more to setting the ignition timing than simply setting the placement of the distributor while the engine is idling.

Back Cover Photos

Top Left: For most performance applications, a distributor is still responsible for triggering the ignition system. Different versions of trigger sources exist and they range from mechanical points to magnetic pickups and Hall-effect switches to light-emitting diodes.

Top Right: The alternator is responsible for keeping everything electrical in your car supplied with the necessary electricity. An alternator must be able to meet and exceed the charging requirements of your car's electrical system in order to keep the battery charged for the next start.

Middle Left: Most aftermarket distributors have the ability to stop the advance. In the case of an MSD distributor, four stop bushings bolt in place under the advance plate. A larger diameter allows less advance.

Middle Right: A distributor test bench allows you to spin the distributor and set up the advance before installing it in your car. Finding one, or even someone who knows how to use it, is getting tough. Companies that specialize in distributors, such as Davis Unified Incorporated, take note of your engine's specs and tune an advance curve to match your needs before sending it to you. Another option is to rent some tuning time on a chassis dyno to get your distributor and power dialed in.

Bottom Left: This chart illustrates the multi-sparking capabilities of most capacitive discharge ignition controls. Each spark is at full output power and the series of sparks generally lasts for 20 degrees of crankshaft rotation.

Bottom Right: When an aftermarket ECU is incorporated, you can choose what coils work best for your application. This land speed racer uses eight MSD compact Blaster SS coils because of their performance, size, and ease of mounting. A MoTech engine controller manages the spark and timing.

OVERSEAS DISTRIBUTION BY:

PGUK
63 Hatton Garden
London EC1N 8LE, England
Phone: 020 7061 1980 • Fax: 020 7242 3725
www.pguk.co.uk.

Renniks Publications Ltd.
3/37-39 Green Street
Banksmeadow, NSW 2109, Australia
Phone: 2 9695 7055 • Fax: 2 9695 7355
www.renniks.com

CONTENTS

S-A DESIGN

PREFACE

Thanks for picking up *High-Performance Ignition Systems*. To many, the automotive ignition system may cause anxiety or be intimidating. For those of you who feel this way, take a deep breath and relax because this book is written in car-guy language (no engineering-speak). I'm merely serving as an interpreter between you and the brains that do comprehend electrons, induction, Henrys, joules, and capacitance. I prefer not to think about all the little things that have to happen on the circuit boards of these controls, and would rather take the time to explain the different parts and accessories you need to assemble and tune a great-performing ignition system.

What makes me qualified to write a book on high-performance ignition systems? I started just like everyone else, as an enthusiast. I also just happened to spend almost two decades involved in the performance-ignition area of the aftermarket with one of the leading companies, MSD Performance, so I picked up a lot of useful information and experience. Now, I get to pass this info on in the hope that it answers a lot of the questions and troubles I've heard about through the years.

Before I got into this industry, I had many of the same questions about ignitions that you probably do. I've stood in speed shops wondering if my mild 454 really needs a 60,000-volt coil. I've cracked my elbow on the hood hinge after grabbing the coil wire and getting shocked. I've introduced the timing light to the cooling fan, burned plug wires, and even shorted out a tach. I've made many of the same mistakes that everyone else has, but maybe won't admit. This book will answer your questions and help you avoid some of those mistakes.

So pull up a stool and kick your feet up on the toolbox and let's bench race about ignitions!

ACKNOWLEDGMENTS

I owe a debt of gratitude to a long list of people who helped me with this project. I also need to thank all of the ignition companies within the aftermarket. Even when I was working as a competitor to some of the companies, everyone was always willing to send images, products for photos, and plenty of technical information. It's refreshing to be in an industry where you can count on your competition to also be your peers. For that, thanks to the team at MSD Performance, Holley, Comp Performance Group, Crane Cams, Mallory, Accel, Granatelli Motorsports, Moroso, Performance Distributors, Electromotive, Pertronix, and more. I hope you find your products represented well throughout.

Of course kudos go to the team at CarTech Inc. for working with me on this project over the years. Special thanks go to my wife, Elizabeth, for her patience and understanding for my need to have multiple projects and deadlines at all times. One less item is on the list now (but probably two more were added).

Author Todd Ryden has a passion for nearly anything on wheels. A Michigan native, he now lives in rust-free El Paso, Texas.

New Hemi or classic Hemi, plenty of options are available to brighten the spark in the cylinder.

Ignition manufacturers almost always offer different levels of ignition products for different levels of performance. Research can help you decide what you need for your application, or you can just call the manufacturer's tech line to see what they recommend.

INTRODUCTION

It's the beginning of the book, so it's perfectly fitting to start with the basics of the ignition system before we get into performance goodies. The goal of an automotive ignition system is to produce a spark that will promote the combustion of the air/fuel mixture in a given cylinder. This is simplified to say the least.

The spark that the ignition produces must have a high enough voltage to jump the spark plug gap. In addition, it must arrive in the cylinder at a near perfect instant in the combustion stroke of the piston. The spark occurs when the air/fuel mixture is being compressed. The mixture is ignited, resulting in a tremendous downforce on the piston that in turn spins the crankshaft. The fact that the ignition system makes this all happen with a high-output spark, thousands of times in a minute, is something most of us take for granted. A great deal of work is taking place behind the scenes, and a lot can cause things to go wrong that will rob your engine of performance. You need to assemble a reliable ignition system that will meet your engine's requirements.

An automotive ignition system operates by taking a low voltage with high current from the car's battery and changing it into a higher voltage with lower current to jump the spark plug gap and induce combustion in the cylinder. This process of changing low voltage to high voltage, called induction, takes place in

the coil. From there, the distributor must get the spark to the correct cylinder at the perfect moment.

Since electricity is not something we can physically hold, the ignition system has always presented a mystery to performance enthusiasts. Once you better understand how the ignition works and what each component actually does, it will begin to make sense. Nothing magical or mysterious is happening in the ignition, although sometimes it may feel that way. Don't let the number of aftermarket CD ignitions, distributors, and coils worry you. Having so many selections available to improve your ignition's performance is a great thing, as it allows you to pick and choose the components that will provide the power you need for your car or truck.

The ignition, as you'll find out, is an integral part of your car's performance. A weak spark will result in

poor combustion and lack of power. Timing issues can also rob power or even cause pre-ignition or detonation. A burned spark plug wire will result in no fire getting to the cylinder. As you read through these chapters, you will see that I explain how different components work and their benefits. This is not meant to be a catalog for ignition components, and I didn't set out to compare or pit one component against another one. If you want to read more about a component's output specs or other features, go to the company's website or get their catalog.

This book is meant to explain the different areas of an automotive ignition and the ways that you can achieve better performance by adding to and tuning your ignition. Once you have a grasp of an ignition's operation, you'll be able to select the parts you need so your engine will perform to its full potential.

Numerous different components go into an ignition system. Your ignition's performance can be enhanced in many ways by selecting components that offer improved accuracy, output, and strength.

ELECTRICAL SYSTEM OVERVIEW

INTRODUCTION TO AUTOMOTIVE IGNITION OPERATION

Let's review a little about electricity itself before getting into the ignition system components. We'll start with electrons that zoom through the wiring of your vehicle

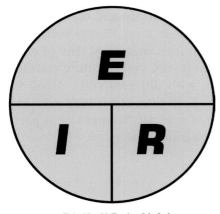

OHM'S LAW

$$\text{(Voltage) } E = I \times R$$
$$\text{(Amps) } I = \frac{E}{R}$$
$$\text{(Ohms) } R = \frac{E}{I}$$

Understanding Ohm's Law gives you a better understanding of how voltage (the pressure), current (the speed), and ohms (the resistance) work together to determine the electrical requirements and circuitry of your car's ignition and electrical system.

and power everything from headlights to radio to the ignition system. The movement, or flow, of the electrons through the system (known as current) is measured in amps and the force required to move them is referred to as voltage. ("Use the force" takes on a whole new meaning now, doesn't it?) The third part of basic electronic circuitry is the resistance against the flow of electrons, which is measured in Ohms.

To wrap your head around this theory, here is a simple comparison using a garden hose. Replace the electrons with water pouring through the hose (the conductor). How far you open the faucet determines the force to push the water that controls the pressure (the voltage). Then, if you kink the hose it produces a resistance (Ohms), which slows the current. Add a couple more resistance kinks and it really slows down the output, unless you increase the force (voltage).

Moving that analogy along and into car-guy speak, say that it's time to fill a bucket to wash your car. Turning the faucet on partway determines the force to push the water

through the hose (amps). How far this faucet is turned on represents 12 volts, and we'll keep it there. If you have the nozzle at the end barely cracked open, it's going to take a while to fill the bucket, but by opening the nozzle wider you reduce the resistance and more water flows (current) to quickly fill the bucket so you can get scrubbing.

Throughout this book, we're going to stick with 12-volt, negative ground electrical systems. Some race applications use 16-volt batteries. That would be like opening the faucet wider to force more water through the hose. Notice the relationship of the three units: voltage, current, and resistance. Current varies in direct proportion to voltage, while it is inversely proportional to resistance. That is, as voltage increases, so does current. However, as resistance increases, current decreases. Those comparisons work into an actual theory, Ohm's Law (after the physicist Georg Ohm). This law helps determine the outcome of the third unit when two are known: electrical voltage (E) equals current (I) multiplied by resistance (R).

System Sides

Before you can plan an ignition system for your engine, you need to understand the fundamentals of a system and each of the main components. An ignition system needs to:

- Distribute the spark to the combustion chamber at the opportune moment in the compression stroke of the piston
- Control and even change the moment that the spark occurs in the cylinder to meet different engine demands
- Be able to reliably accomplish these goals throughout a variety of operating conditions and changing temperatures

A car's ignition system and its components can be broken down into two sides: primary and secondary.

The Primary Side

The primary side consists of components that operate with the low voltage from the battery. Note that all of these parts use conventional wiring, since they're carrying lower voltages. This includes the battery itself, the ignition switch, a switching device, an ignition control (when used), and the wiring leading to the coil's negative and positive terminals. The coil is the point at which the primary and secondary systems meet; a low voltage goes into the coil, but a high voltage comes out through the high-tension lead.

The Secondary Side

The high-voltage lead that comes out of the coil, known as the coil wire, is connected to the distributor cap. From there, the high voltage, generally anywhere from 20,000 to

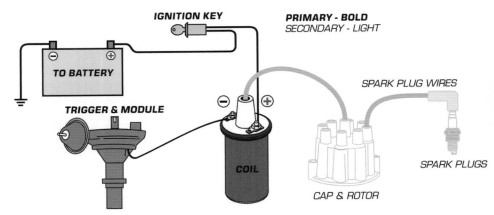

This chart shows a complete ignition system with the primary components in bold and the secondary components in gray. The primary side consists of components that deal with lower voltages, while the secondary deals with at least 15,000 volts and much higher voltages in performance applications.

40,000 volts, races through the rotor tip and across a small gap to another cap terminal. From there it moves out of the cap, through a spark plug wire, and finally across the spark plug gap. The secondary side of the ignition requires high-voltage wiring with thick insulation: the spark plug wires. All of the components that make up the secondary side of the ignition are maintenance items and need to be checked throughout the cruising or racing season.

The Coil

The ignition coil is an incredible part of the ignition system; it's the system's magical black box. Think about it. The coil receives 12 volts from the battery and then outputs a spark of at least 15,000 volts. Once you understand how this phenomenon works, you can tune your ignition with different coils. A coil falls into both sides of the ignition system but is generally thought of as part of the secondary side.

Many shapes and sizes of coils are available for a variety of different ignitions. Engineers can manipulate the internals of coils to make higher voltage, increased current, different spark duration, and more. Be sure to choose a coil to match your needs.

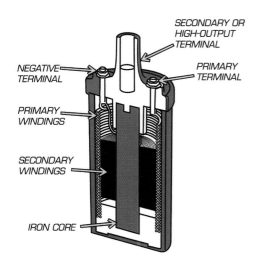

This cutaway shows the internals of a canister coil. The main components are a set of primary windings, an iron core to promote the magnetic field created, and a set of secondary windings.

The coil consists of two sets of windings made up of insulated wires surrounding an iron core. The primary windings are generally made up of several hundred turns of a heavy wire. The secondary windings are made up of a much smaller-gauge wire and consist of thousands of turns.

Coil manufacturers use the ratio between the number of secondary and primary windings as a specification. For example, 100:1 means 100 secondary turns to every 1 turn of the primary. This is a commonly used specification that can be useful in your search to locate the best coil for your application.

When the switching device or trigger signal is closed in a typical factory-style inductive ignition (see Chapter 4), current from the battery flows through the thicker primary windings and a magnetic field builds in strength thanks to the help of the iron core.

When the switching device opens (or is triggered), the flow of current is broken and its magnetic field collapses over to the thousands of secondary windings. During this collapse, the voltage is increased, creating the higher voltage that is required to jump the spark plug gap and ignite the air/fuel mixture.

Distributor

Like the coil, the distributor dabbles a little into the primary side of the ignition, but is very important and probably best known for its role in distributing the higher secondary voltage. The distributor generally houses the trigger mechanism that controls when the primary voltage collapses to the secondary windings of the coil.

Before any of this occurs, though, the distributor shaft must be turned. In most cases, this is done by the engine's camshaft. Two helically cut gears mesh together to turn the distributor shaft. This rotation starts the triggering, centrifugal advance (when equipped), high-voltage acceptance from the coil, and subsequent delivery through the cap's terminals. From there, the voltage travels through the spark plug wires and eventually reaches the plugs.

There's a lot riding on and in the distributor, so pay attention when you're looking to upgrade.

Trigger Device

The several ways to trigger the ignition all have the same goal: to break the flow of current into the coil, resulting in a high voltage induced into the secondary side of the coil. This triggering can be accomplished through mechanical breaker points or electronic variations. The example of conventional breaker points is the easiest way to explain the operation of triggering the ignition.

Think of the breaker points as a simple open/closed switch that is

Most distributors are responsible for triggering the ignition as well as carrying the high voltage to the cylinders at the correct time. Before electronics controlled the timing, the distributor handled that chore as well.

Distributorless Systems

Have you ever stopped to wonder how all of the trigger signals, timing, and delivery of spark would occur if there were no distributor at all? That's right, no distributor. Actually, new cars don't use distributors anymore. However, most hot rods and traditional domestic performance engines use a distributor (although the late-model Hemi, Coyote, and LS engines are challenging that).

As electronic engine management system development progressed, the roles of the distributor continued to diminish until they completely disappeared. The majority of racing and performance cars still use distributors, which is why I include them throughout this discussion. However, the distributorless contingent is growing. Both systems still need a trigger source and electronics to control the charging and operation of the coils, whether it's through the distributor or through an electronic control unit (ECU) and electronic ignition module.

Several variations of the distributorless ignition systems (DIS) are available. Coil pack models have a coil with two towers and fire two cylinders. These have a variety of ignition upgrades available. Other versions have a coil for every cylinder. The latest systems even have the coil mounted right to the spark plug with no spark plug wire. Some companies even specialize in an entire system that allows you to obsolete your own distributor.

Whatever type of ignition system your engine sports, they all have shared traits, including what it takes to upgrade their performance.

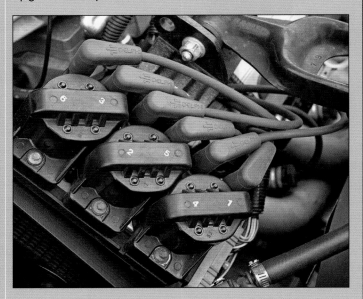

Even if your engine doesn't have a distributor, the theory of a distributor-triggered ignition system remains. Instead of a trigger from the distributor going to the coil, a signal from a crankshaft sensor is responsible for triggering the coil's high voltage.

For most performance applications, a distributor is still responsible for triggering the ignition system. Different versions of trigger sources exist and they range from mechanical points to magnetic pickups and Hall-effect switches to light-emitting diodes.

Detroit Goes Electronic

Each of the Big Three domestic auto manufacturers had their own electronic ignition system by the mid-1970s.

Chrysler

Chrysler was the first when it installed electronic ignitions as standard equipment across the board in 1973. The system used a magnetic pickup in the distributor with a small electronic controller to manage the dwell and flow of current to the coil. This system has gone through variations over the years, but for the most part the same system is still offered today.

The distributor trigger is the same, and there have probably been changes in the mechanical advance setup, but the real difference in design is in the ignition boxes for different performance applications. Chrysler didn't want to be bothered with exciting marketing names, so they simply offer three different colors: orange, gold, and chrome. The Orange box is the basic street version; the Gold is the high-output race system, and the Chrome box somewhere in between.

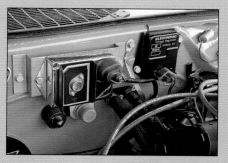

Chrysler was the first of the Big Three to move from breaker points to electronics. They were also the first OEM to offer high-output ignition modules, and they still offer them under the Mopar Performance Parts banner. The Chrome ignition module is a step up in performance from the Orange model.

Ford

Ford introduced the Duraspark electronic ignition in 1974, which (like the Chrysler design) used a magnetic pickup with an external ignition controller. In the later 1970s, this system was upgraded with components to improve the secondary voltage and longevity of the parts, including a larger-diameter distributor cap. This upgrade was officially dubbed Duraspark II.

These distributors are still supplied on many of Ford's performance crate engines. Ford also offers an Extra Performance Ignition Module that delivers increased spark energy and even has a built-in rev limiter.

General Motors

The first mass-produced electronic distributor from General Motors was the High Energy Ignition (HEI) unitized distributor. HEI was on every GM product by 1975. Not only did this distributor incorporate a magnetic pickup design, but it also had the coil incorporated into its cap. Although the distributor is bulky, it offers a single-wire hookup, and there are no external components or other wiring. These benefits have kept the GM HEI system extremely popular among enthusiasts, and it is still widely used and supplied in many of GM crate motors.

GM's integrated coil-in-cap distributor, known as the HEI, was a breakthrough in electronic distributor technology. They're still in use today and even mandated in some forms of circle track racing. You can find an assortment of performance parts and brand-new HEI distributors for applications from street rods to racing.

normally closed. While in the closed position, voltage from the battery flows into the primary windings because the closed points are providing a path to ground. When the points open, all of the current in the coil jumps to the secondary windings, where it eventually finds a ground path through the spark plug. As soon as the points close again, the original ground path is returned and the battery current flows through the primary again. The time when the points are closed is called the dwell time.

Breaker points haven't been used in new cars for years, but they are still available in new aftermarket distributors. Electronic triggers that offer maintenance-free operation and improved trigger control replaced breaker points in the mid-1970s.

All trigger designs share the common goal of signaling the ignition to release the high-voltage spark; they just take different routes to get there. In most cases, the trigger device is located inside the distributor, but there are exceptions.

Most high-end drag cars and many late-model cars have systems that incorporate an external trigger device on the crankshaft. This is commonly called a crank trigger. Even late-model systems that don't have a distributor still require a switching method. Beyond mechanical breaker points, much better electronic trigger devices exist that do not wear or require adjusting, including magnetic pickups, Hall-effect switches, and optical triggers (see Chapter 2 for more details).

Timing

As with so many things in life, when you're dealing with ignition systems, timing is everything. The

Moving the distributor (when it holds the trigger device) can control the ignition's trigger. However, there is much more to setting the ignition timing than simply setting the placement of the distributor while the engine is idling.

spark must jump the spark plug gap at the exact moment in order to achieve the best combustion event, and thus the most force to push the piston down on the power stroke. If the spark occurs too late (is too retarded) in the compression stroke, the air/fuel mixture may not have enough time to fully combust, resulting in less force to push the piston. If the spark occurs too soon, the combustion event may occur too early, resulting in pre-ignition, which robs the engine of power and can even lead to damage. Pre-ignition is sometimes referred to as detonation.

To make matters worse, the ideal timing setting varies as engine RPM and load change. At low RPM, the piston is traveling slower, so you need less time to burn the fuel at high RPM: The fuel must be ignited sooner in the piston's stroke to achieve the same burn. This can be done mechanically inside the distributor, or with numerous electronic controls.

When the distributor is saddled with this chore, it is equipped with a mechanical advance assembly that operates through centrifugal force. Controlling how fast and how far the timing advances is another aspect of tuning. While we're inside the distributor, this is another chore to add to its list of responsibilities. Whether or not the distributor triggers the ignition, it still has to perform the task for which it was named.

The distributor has the job of sending the spark from the coil to each of the spark plugs. This is done through the rotor and the cap. The high voltage from the coil enters the cap through its center terminal. This terminal is made out of a long-lasting, highly conductive material, because it is in constant contact with the rotor tang. It is different from the other terminals as it has a ball or tip inside the cap.

The rotor tang is generally bent up and away from the base of the rotor. This is either the entire rotor tip, or it joins into a thicker material for better spark transfer. Watch for excessive pitting or signs of burning on the rotor tang.

When the rotor tip aligns with the distributor cap terminal, the spark should jump across to the terminal. Once the spark makes it across to the cap terminals, it's a simple run through the spark plug wire to the spark plug and across its gap. As with any path, there may be obstacles along the way.

Spark Plug Wires

The importance of good-quality spark plug wires cannot be stressed enough. Spark plug wires are the arteries of the ignition system, as they provide a path for the sparks to get to the spark plugs. Plug wires need to be able to live in a harsh environment and deal with high heat, abrasion, and getting whipped around at high speeds. They also need to be able to deliver high voltage levels, while suppressing electromagnetic interference (EMI), which is created when high voltage passes through a wire.

EMI can be an annoying buzz on your radio and is known as radio noise. It can also wreak havoc on other electronics within your vehicle such as the RPM limiter, or even the ECU of a car equipped with an electronic fuel-injection (EFI) system. OEM spark plug wires combat EMI by using a carbon-core material that has a very high resistance to the flow of energy. These are fine for stock-performing daily drivers, but when it comes to high-performance ignition systems, a wire with lower resistance and high EMI suppression capability is needed.

Another area of importance in a spark plug wire is the crimp between the terminal and the wire. Poor crimps can contribute to intermittent performance, a dead cylinder, and other problems.

Also pay attention to the spark plug wire boots. They need to survive in their close proximity to the exhaust manifolds where heat is at its most extreme.

This distributor cutaway shows the relationship of the rotor tip and the distributor cap terminal post. This is another gap across which the spark must jump. The cap and rotor need to be inspected periodically.

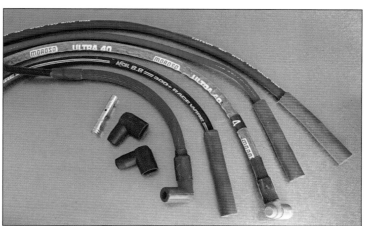

Plug wires play a critical role in the ignition system. Wires need to be able to handle extreme underhood temperatures and the high voltage and current that the ignition produces. If a wire fails, you feel it.

Spark Plugs

The final leap that the spark needs to take is across the gap of the spark plug itself. The spark transfers from the plug wire terminal to the threaded tip of the plug's center terminal. This center terminal reaches all the way through the ceramic shell of the plug and ends at the electrode. The gap is between the electrode and the metal housing of the plug. The metal housing forms a ground to the engine. The voltage jumps the gap to the electrode. The resulting spark ignites the air/fuel mixture in the cylinder, and the ignition cycle starts all over for the next cylinder in the firing order.

Each spark plug manufacturer has its own theories on why one is better than the other. Versions include platinum-tipped plugs, plugs with tiny electrodes, plugs with numerous electrodes, and more. Also available are resistor plugs, nonresistor plugs, hot plugs, and cold plugs.

Another area of spark plug design that can affect the engine's performance is the size of the spark plug gap. Opening the gap forces the coil to build a higher voltage so the spark can jump the gap. The engine's compression and cylinder pressures affect gap size.

High cylinder pressure from nitrous or forced induction places limits on the plug gap. Too large a gap also puts added pressure on the secondary side of the ignition system, resulting in shortening the life of the components. Too small a gap can result in the spark not being strong enough to create a full combustion cycle of the air/fuel mixture.

Ignition Controls

One of the most popular ways to upgrade an ignition's output is by wiring in an external capacitive discharge (CD) ignition control. You've probably seen these controls at shows, races, and in magazines.

If your car is firing on the stock ignition system, adding one of these controls is an easy and effective way to improve performance. Most of these controls are wired to the primary side of the ignition and deliver a much hotter spark to the coil. They can also enhance the dwell control, resulting in big spark improvements on the secondary side.

Obviously, a factory ignition system doesn't require an aftermarket ignition control, although many aftermarket distributors do.

Battery and Charging System

Unless your engine uses a magneto, you need a battery to get the engine fired up, and to supply the ignition with current and voltage created by the alternator. The battery is the main power storage for a performance ignition system. It is kept at capacity thanks to an alternator.

The alternator is really what keeps the electrical and ignition systems of your car operating by creating electricity. The battery is more like a gas tank and provides the means to get the system started again once the engine is turned off. Your alternator must be up to the task of creating more electricity than your car (including headlights, ignition, brake lights, AC, etc.) will ever need.

Alternators are used on all street cars and, today, even on the majority of race engines. The alternator is responsible for producing the electricity that a car draws out of the battery while the car is running. The crankshaft is connected to a belt and pulley that turns the alternator that then generates an alternating

Spark plugs are the final step in the ignition process. As with most of the ignition system, a lot of different plugs are available, but they all serve the same purpose: to light the fuel mixture.

An aftermarket ignition control can spice up your stock ignition's output. Many different controls are available to cover almost any ignition system, including distributorless. This is just one of Mallory's capacitive discharge ignition controls.

The battery is critical to your ignition system's performance, not to mention anything that runs off electricity on your car. Think of the battery as a fuel tank for the ignition; it must always be charged and at the ready.

The alternator is responsible for keeping everything electrical in your car supplied with the necessary electricity. An alternator must be able to meet and exceed the charging requirements of your car's electrical system in order to keep the battery charged for the next start.

current (AC). With the engine running, a rotor is spun inside the alternator that creates a magnetic field. This field is induced into the windings of a stator, and eventually makes its way to the battery. If you run a battery without a charging system, it is important that it's fully charged at the beginning of the race so that it has the capacity to power all of the car's electrical needs through to the finish line.

More than just the ignition system relies on the battery. The starter is also gulping huge amounts of current to turn over your street or race engine. Other electrical devices such as fans, pumps, motors, and even fuel injection controls all tap into the battery for voltage, which is why the alternator needs to be able to keep up with the demands of the electrical system.

The Sum of the Parts

As you can see, the ignition system has several key components and all of them work together to produce a spark and deliver it at the right moment in the engine cycle. If one part isn't up to its task, the entire system suffers. If the rotor is worn, for example, the spark isn't going to make it to the plugs. If the coil is shorted out, its spark output is going to suffer. Therefore, it is important that the entire system is assembled and wired correctly from the start and kept in check with thorough maintenance.

A variety of ignition systems and components are available for your performance car, truck, or whatever you race. Each component has its pros and cons, but all components share the same ultimate goal: to create combustion.

DISTRIBUTOR BASICS
TRIGGERS, TIMING ADVANCE AND DELIVERY

In most factory-type ignitions from before the mid 1990s, the ignition cycle begins and ends with the distributor. One might say that the ignition goes full circle around the distributor.

The majority of cars being modified and updated for performance and racing today still use a distributor to trigger the ignition system (although that number is losing ground to coil-per-cylinder technology). Alternatives, such as crank-triggered ignitions, are available and they show up more on higher-performance race applications. However, these still require a distributor to deliver the sparks.

The use of distributorless electronic ignitions continues to grow, thanks in part to OEMs and several aftermarket manufacturers that offer high-performance components for a growing number of applications (see Chapter 8 for more details).

This chapter concentrates on the workings of the run-of-the-mill automotive distributor and its functions. This type of distributor has the following characteristics and responsibilities:

- It incorporates some sort of trigger device.
- It has the ability to alter the timing throughout changes in RPM and engine conditions.

- It distributes the spark to the correct plug terminal at the right moment.
- Most are also responsible for driving the oil pump in the engine.

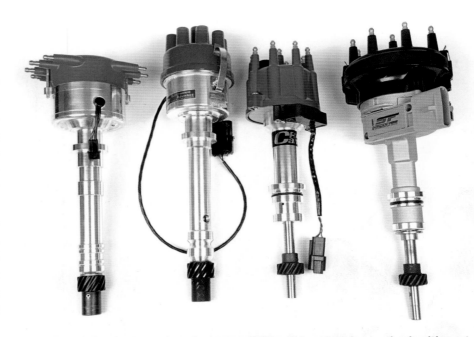

The distributor carries a lot of responsibility. It has to trigger the ignition at the exact moment, meet the changing needs of the engine, and then deliver the spark to the correct spark plug. Over the years, different trigger methods have been developed. The overall methodology of a distributor has remained much the same despite advances in trigger systems, mechanical advances, and materials.

Distributing the Spark

The distributor is responsible for distributing the spark from the ignition coil to the appropriate cylinder via its cap and the plug wires. To do this, the distributor shaft is driven by the camshaft through helically cut gears with a 1:1 ratio (the distributor matches one revolution of the camshaft). On most engines, the oil pump is driven off the distributor shaft. This is accomplished through an intermediate shaft connecting the distributor shaft at or below these gears. At the top of the distributor shaft is the rotor.

The high secondary voltage released by the coil is sent through the high-tension coil wire to the center terminal of the distributor cap. The end of this terminal has a carbon ball inside the distributor cap that is in contact with the center of the rotor's spring contact. This leads to a copper or brass tip that extends from the center to the rotor's outer edge. As the rotor spins, the voltage transfers over a small gap to the distributor cap terminal when they align. Then the voltage shoots through the spark plug wire and to the spark plug, where it ionizes across the gap and ignites the air/fuel mixture. It sounds easy enough, but plenty can go wrong.

OEM distributors were made from an aluminum casting and even plastic (or steel and iron way back when) and then fit with a bushing to support the shaft. Over time, this bushing wears and may cause the shaft to wobble in the housing. Any wobble or worn areas can and do affect the timing. Top-of-the-line performance aftermarket distributors are generally CNC machined from billet aluminum to form a strong and non-porous housing. Inside, a roller

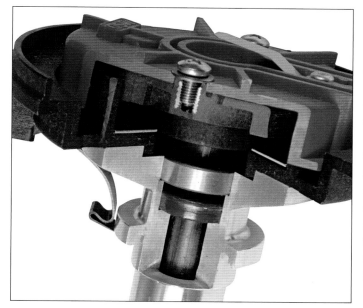

The majority of OEM distributors had bushings to guide the shaft. Most of the new aftermarket billet aluminum distributors feature a ball or needle-bearing guide in the top housing. Some models have a bearing at the bottom also, or they use an extra-long bushing.

Some aftermarket billet aluminum distributors can provide improved oil flow to the distributor gear. Optional O-rings on Chevrolet models help control the oil flow by sealing off the lifter gallery. These O-rings can only be used when the block has been modified. This modification involves chamfering the upper and lower edges of the distributor hole in the block.

or ball bearing usually supports the distributor shaft. This design ensures smooth and accurate control of the distributor shaft.

If you cannot find a performance aftermarket distributor for your rare engine, or if you are a numbers-matching muscle-car fanatic and insist on using the stock distributor, make sure it spins true and that there is no excessive wobble or end play. There are still places where you

can get new bushings or a new shaft installed to tighten up that original distributor. Search the pages of *Hemmings Motor News* or other specialist vehicle publications or websites.

Triggering the Ignition

The distributor must also trigger the ignition or coil. Several different methods will accomplish the trigger, including mechanical

One answer to insufficient coil saturation time from points is the dual-point distributor. Each set is precisely positioned with one slightly staggered. In this setup, the first set is just closing as the second set is opening. The result is increased dwell time to ensure full spark delivery at higher RPM.

Millions of breaker-points distributors have been produced and are still switching away on many cars. This worn distributor belongs in a 283-ci Chevrolet. The points are simply an on/off controller for the coil.

This illustration shows the operation of a breaker-points distributor. When it is closed, the coil is building up current in its primary windings. When the points open, this field collapses to the secondary windings, creating a high-voltage spark that is delivered to the distributor and spark plug wires. Opening the points too far diminishes the dwell.

Breaker Points

Points systems are still being used in many cars, and you can still get a brand-new aftermarket distributor with points. The quantity of these distributors really isn't that out of order when you consider how many vehicles were produced with points providing the trigger. After all, it was the early 1970s before electronic triggers and systems phased out points. These days, finding a new set of points at the local auto parts store is getting tougher, and so is finding a counterman who understands what you're looking for. Nevertheless, points are still used and actually get the job done fairly well to a certain degree.

Like the distributor itself, breaker points received their name directly from their vocation: breaking a circuit. That circuit is the primary current going into the coil by opening its ground path. The path that is broken is the lead that goes from the coil negative terminal to the points. When the points are closed, current is delivered to the coil primary windings, creating a magnetic field. When the points open (break the ground circuit), this field collapses to the secondary windings and a spark is sent out of the coil to the spark plugs.

breaker points, electronic switching devices such as a magnetic pickup or Hall-effect switch, and optical triggers. Whichever triggering path you follow, the goal is the same: to trigger the high voltage from the coil and to get it to the spark plugs at the perfect moment in the compression stroke of each cylinder.

Adjusting and Setting Points

When adjusting the points gap on a bench, a new set should be opened slightly wider than a used set. As a rule, for a V-8 engine, a new set should be opened to approximately .018 to .020 inch, while a used set could be about .014 to .017 inch. New points are set a touch wider to accommodate the rubbing block seating into the distributor cam. This should only be done to get the gap close; using a dwell meter, check the dwell and adjust it with the engine running. It is recommended that you review your shop manual for the proper specification because applications vary among manufacturers.

People who have a dwell meter, and know how to use it, are becoming scarce. A dwell meter simply connects to 12 volts and ground from the battery, and has a lead that connects to the negative terminal of the coil. Here the dwell is set at approximately 32 degrees. Perfect!

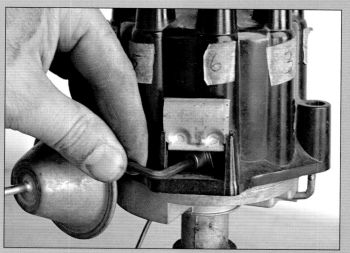

As a rule, the dwell should be set between 28 and 32 degrees. It can be adjusted through the window of the distributor cap by moving the Allen-head screw that adjusts the position of the breaker arm on GM applications.

On the distributor shaft in a V-8 engine, there is a cam with eight flat areas and eight lobes. The switching arm of the points is spring-loaded and has a rubbing block that rides against the cam. Each time a lobe comes up, it pushes the rubbing block, which opens the points contact and creates the trigger signal. When this happens, the rotor tip is also aligned with the distributor cap terminal to transfer the voltage to the spark plug wire.

Breaker points were used for decades and you really can't deny their ability to get the job done. However, they do have shortcomings. For starters, they are mechanical, which means they require adjustment, and they wear over time. Excessive wear or poor adjustment eventually has an adverse effect on the timing and quality of the spark. Points were designed to handle a small amount of current, which limits their potential output. In addition, points tend to bounce at higher racing RPM, with the result that the points burn and the ignition misses.

Dwell time is measured in the number of degrees of the distributor's rotation through which the points contacts are closed. This is the coil saturation time. This is the time during which the coil produces the strong magnetic field that creates the high-voltage spark to fire across the spark plug gap. If the points open too much, the dwell time is reduced, and the voltage output of the coil is weak. This could cause a misfire under loads. If the dwell time is too long (the gap doesn't open as much), an arc may occur across the contact points resulting in failure of the points, as well as poor coil output. Adjusting dwell time is known as setting the dwell.

What's the Point?

I have mentioned some downsides to points, but there are cases when you can keep them. At least you can keep your numbers-matching distributor and improve the performance of the ignition. Not every car needs a billet aluminum distributor. You can get by on a good-working, accurate distributor for a weekend cruiser or a vehicle that isn't revved up to redline constantly.

Points still have their place, but a magnetic pickup distributor is much more accurate than a points distributor. A magnetic pickup distributor is especially so when complemented with an adjustable advance, sealed bearings, and a billet housing.

In order to accomplish this, make sure that the distributor is in good working order. The bushings should be solid and there should be no wobble or excessive endplay. In addition, the mechanical advance should be in accurate working order and set up properly for your engine. While you're at it, you may want to check out the vacuum advance.

You can easily upgrade your stock points distributor to an electronic trigger with a kit from Pertronix. A Hall-effect switch mounts in place of the breaker points and a ring with eight magnets installs under the mechanical advance plate. Pertronix has these points-to-electronics kits available for most applications.

Options

If the distributor checks out okay, what are your options? If you just can't handle the thought of having old breaker-point technology under the distributor cap, you can easily replace the points with an electronic trigger kit such as one offered by Pertronix or Crane.

Pertronix Kits

Pertronix offers the Ignitor and Ignitor II kits that provide an easy way to install a Hall-effect pickup as an alternative to points. These kits feature a thin reluctor wheel that has a magnet for each cylinder. This reluctor installs on the bottom of the advance plate, just beneath the rotor. The points assembly and condenser are removed and replaced with a Hall-effect pickup.

Two wires come from the Ignitor pickup and connect to the coil's positive terminal (where it receives 12 volts) and the coil's negative terminal. Just like that, you have an electronic ignition that produces more voltage than the points ever did, plus it's maintenance free. The Ignitor II produces even more energy and voltage, so you receive the benefits of a hotter spark as well as never having to adjust the points again.

Crane's XR-i points replacement kit simply bolts in place of the points and uses the original cam wheel. An added bonus is that it has a built-in adjustable rev limiter.

Crane Module

Crane offers an electronic module that simply replaces the points. It uses the stock cam on the distributor to produce its trigger signal. The unit is digitally controlled and is almost too simple to believe.

A really trick feature of this module is a built-in RPM limiter. You can get rid of the points in your restored muscle car and have the protection of an over-rev limiter as well.

CD Ignition Control

The final option is to bite the breaker-points bullet and realize that you never zinged the engine into points float to begin with. You can easily wire in a CD ignition control, such as a 6-Series from Crane, Mallory, or MSD, and use the points to trigger it. You get all the benefits of the high-energy multiple sparks, plus the points will probably never need to be replaced again. (See Chapter 4 for more details.)

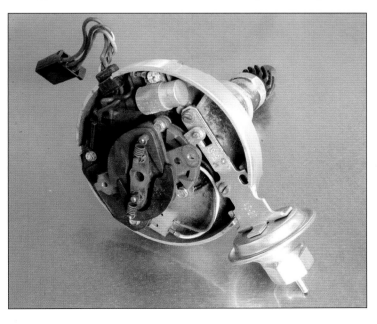

The GM HEI distributor is still a popular choice for many enthusiasts, thanks to its one-wire installation and internal coil. In fact, they're popular enough that Davis Unified Incorporated offers them to fit Ford and Chrysler engines in a variety of performance levels.

Another important component within a points system is the condenser. When the contact points open, the condenser ensures a clean break of the current flow. This causes the current to move out of the coil rather than across the points gap. If the condenser is faulty, the points show premature and excessive burning. If the condenser is shorted, it causes a no-start condition. Condensers rarely fail or cause trouble, so you don't hear too much about these issues, but they perform an important function.

Electronic Ignition Triggers

In the early 1970s, electronic triggers were creeping into OEM distributors. Chrysler got there and Ford soon followed. They both opted to use a magnetic pickup in their distributors, complemented by an external ignition module. The ignition module is responsible for controlling the dwell time and switching the high voltage.

The first mass-produced electronic distributor from General Motors was the HEI unitized distributor, which was in every GM product by 1975. Not only did this distributor incorporate a magnetic pickup design but it also had the coil incorporated into its cap.

Although the distributor was quite bulky, it offered a single wire

The inside of an HEI distributor doesn't look much different than a points distributor. There is still a mechanical advance, a vacuum canister, and even a condenser. However, the diameter of the distributor is much wider.

hookup and it had no other external components or wiring. These benefits have kept the GM HEI extremely popular among enthusiasts, and they are still widely used and are even supplied in many current GM crate engines. Companies such as Performance Distributors offer performance modules and components to update original models.

GM has used three different designs of the HEI distributor over the years. The first version (and most popular) used a module with four terminals, a centrifugal advance, and a vacuum canister. The aftermarket primarily offers four-pin modules that produce a stronger spark. As more electronics made their way into cars, the HEI eventually lost the vacuum canister. These distributors used a module with seven terminals and controlled the spark timing and vacuum advance.

For a short while, a five-pin module was used. It had very limited timing control, although the vacuum canister was still present. Hot rod and race applications generally use the four-pin design rather than the five- and seven-pin modules. All of these versions use the same style of pickup and mechanical advance.

Going with an aftermarket module and coil is the best way to boost the output of your HEI. High-output ignition modules are offered by most of the performance ignition companies and some are even fit with an adjustable rev limiter.

One thing to check before you add components to your HEI is to make sure that it receives a solid 12 to 14 volts and that the supply wire is at least 14 gauge. The system can't produce high voltage if it doesn't have enough power supply to work with.

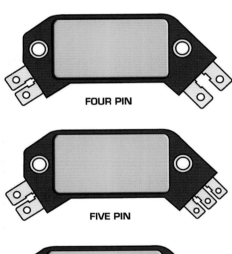

FOUR PIN

FIVE PIN

SEVEN PIN

The number of terminals in GM HEI modules has changed throughout the years. The four-pin module is from the first generation of HEI modules and is the model for which most aftermarket companies offer performance replacement modules. The five- and seven-pin modules incorporated only minor timing control operation that limits their use in the performance realm.

Pickups

The use of an electronic ignition trigger has many benefits. First, of course, is the absence of mechanically moving components, which means that there are no adjustments or parts to wear. In addition, breaker points limit the amount of primary current that can be used. Electronically triggered ignitions can work with higher amperage and voltage and produce higher secondary output. This translates to a hotter spark to help improve combustion, equating to increased power.

Electronic triggers are only responsible for producing a trigger signal. Whether it uses a magnetic pickup or a Hall-effect switch, there still must be an ignition module of some sort that controls the dwell time. This control can be accomplished by different methods, such as with a small module inside the distributor (GM HEI distributor) or with an external box (Ford Duraspark or Chrysler system).

These methods are all inductive ignition systems. They use electronic circuitry and engine RPM to derive predetermined dwell times. There are several types of electronic pickups used in distributors. They share common traits and complete the same task, but do it differently.

Magnetic Pickup: When electronic ignitions replaced breaker points, magnetic pickups were the choice of most OEMs. They have only two wires to connect and are accurate

A magnetic pickup is a compact and simple device. It's accurate, reliable, and never requires adjustment. It does require some sort of electronic device to control the flow of voltage and current through the coil.

and reliable because of this. They are the most popular form of electronic trigger today.

This type of pickup consists of a magnet that has a small wire wound around it to create a mag- netic field, similar to an ignition coil. This pickup is mounted into a trig- ger plate on the base of the distribu- tor. A metal trigger wheel, generally referred to as a reluctor, is mounted to the distributor shaft.

The reluctor has a tab or paddle for each cylinder and spins past the stationary magnetic pickup. Every time one of these paddles passes the pickup assembly, a voltage signal is created that is used to trigger the

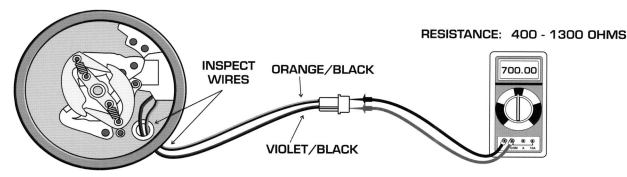

RESISTANCE: 400 - 1300 OHMS

INSPECT WIRES — ORANGE/BLACK

VIOLET/BLACK

CHECKING THE MAGNETIC PICKUP

Checking the resistance of your distributor's magnetic pickup is about the only form of troubleshooting you can do with- out an oscilloscope. The resistance of most aftermarket magnetic pickups should be between 400 and 1,300 ohms. Be sure to check the terminals for a tight, clean connection. Most problems are caused by poor connections or crimp issues.

Magnetic Pickup Polarity

If you are running an MSD ignition control with a mag- netic pickup and you are not sure about the polarity, you can connect the wires and check the timing of the engine. Then swap the position of the wires and check the timing again. You'll notice that the timing changes significantly and may appear erratic.

When used with an analog ignition control the cor- rect connection is when the timing is most retarded. How- ever, if you're using a digitally controlled MSD, the correct polarity connection is when the timing is advanced. The difference is due to differences of the input circuit used in the two ignitions. Depending on the brand of distributor or ignition, the polarity and ignition compatibility can vary, so check with the manufacturer.

PICKUP	POLARITY POSITIVE	POLARITY NEGATIVE
MSD Distributor	Black/Orange	Black/Violet
Accell 46/4800 Series	Black/Orange	Black/Violet
Accell 51/6100 Series	Red	Black
Chrysler Distributor	White/Orange	Black
Ford Distributor	Black/Orange	Black/Violet
GM Distributor	White	Green
MSD Ignition Control	Violet	Green
Moroso Crank Trigger Pickup	White	Black
MSD Crank Trigger Pickup	Violet	Green
Mallory Crank Trigger Pickup	Violet	Green
Hayes Stinger	Black/Green	Black

This chart shows the polarity of several com- mon magnetic pickups. If the wires are connected backward, the ignition timing is inconsistent and the engine runs rough. Depending on what kind of ignition control you use, the timing may appear retarded or advanced.

coil or ignition. As the edge of the paddle lines up with the pickup, it creates negative voltage. When the paddle passes through the signal, the voltage signal becomes positive.

This voltage output increases with the RPM of the engine, making it less susceptible to electronic interference and therefore extremely reliable.

The two wires of a magnetic pickup have polarity, so they can only be connected one way. Therefore it is important to know which wire is positive and which is negative.

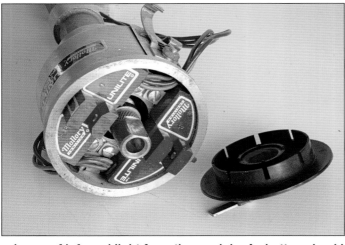

Mallory offers a variety of distributors with breaker points, magnetic pickups, and optical trigger devices. The popular Unilite distributors use a photo coupler that receives a beam of infrared light from the module. A shutter wheel breaks the light beam, producing the trigger signal that tells electronic circuitry to fire the stored energy from the coil. This example carries two Unilite modules to incorporate a redundant ignition system. Such a setup is popular in circle track racing.

Hall-effect switches were used in Ford's TFI ignition modules from the late 1980s and into the 1990s. The Ford design incorporated a stationary magnet. A shudder wheel that blocks the magnetic field turns off the switch. Once it passes, the switch is turned on again by the recurring magnetic field.

Magnetic Pickup Wiring

The magnetic pickup wire routing is important to your engine's performance. Because a magnetic pickup produces a voltage signal to trigger the ignition, it is imperative that the wires are routed away from other wiring, electrical components, the primary coil leads, and spark plug wires. This helps prevent chances of interference that could cause a false or erratic trigger signal. This is especially important in today's performance world with aftermarket EFI systems, electric water pumps, and so on.

Magnetic pickup wires should be twisted together to help create a field around the wires for protection. Also try to route the pickup wiring as close as possible to the engine block, frame, or chassis of the car. These parts serve as large ground planes, so there is less electrical activity near their surfaces.

For the ultimate protection, you can make a shielded harness that provides a grounded shield around the wires. MSD offers a 6-foot shielded harness (PN 8862) that is recommended on high-performance applications, especially with EFI.

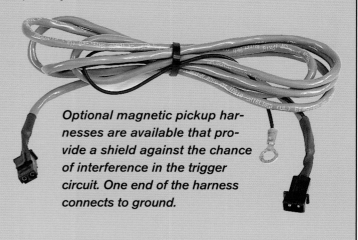

Optional magnetic pickup harnesses are available that provide a shield against the chance of interference in the trigger circuit. One end of the harness connects to ground.

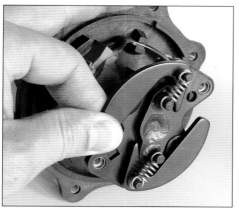

The centrifugal advance assembly is mounted on top of the distributor shaft on most aftermarket models, even Ford distributors. This makes it very easy to change the advance springs to alter the rate of advance; you have better control and the ability to make easier total-timing adjustments.

The operation of a centrifugal advance assembly is simple, yet very important to your engine's performance. As the distributor spins, the weights overcome the tension of the springs and push out from the center of the distributor. This advances the trigger function of the distributor.

You can get advance kits for most distributors with different tension springs and sometimes even different weights. The bushings of different diameters are used to stop the advance at a certain amount in many aftermarket distributors.

When troubleshooting a no-start condition, check the resistance of the pickup. It is very rare for a magnetic pickup to fail, because of the simple construction and lack of moving components. However, stranger things have happened.

Hall-Effect Pickup: Instead of creating its own voltage to use as a trigger signal (as a magnetic pickup does), a Hall-effect switch receives constant power from a positive voltage source (usually 12-volt). A magnet is used to lower (turn off) or raise (turn on) this voltage to produce a trigger signal. This system creates a square wave signal that remains at the same amplitude throughout the RPM range of the engine.

Different methods can be employed to accomplish the switching with a Hall-effect pickup design. Typically, the Hall-effect switch is mounted inside the distributor, on the outer edge of the housing, and a magnet is permanently mounted just inside the switch to create a magnetic field.

Like the reluctor used with a magnetic pickup, a Hall-effect device incorporates a shutter wheel that either opens or closes to block the magnetic field between the pickup and magnet. When the two are blocked off, there is no magnetic field, which

means the switch is turned off. When the window of the wheel passes the magnet and becomes aligned again with the sensor, a magnetic field is created and the switch is turned on.

The shutter wheel of a Hall-effect system has eight openings and closings for each cylinder (six for a six-cylinder, four on four-cylinders). The benefit of this trigger system is that it produces a constant voltage signal, since the device is turned on and off, rather than switching from a negative to a positive voltage. A Hall-effect switch is extremely accurate. It has one extra power wire to connect and costs a little more than a magnetic pickup.

Optical Pickup: This well-known electronic trigger device is also called a photo-optic system. It is a derivative of a Hall-effect switch because it also incorporates a shutter wheel that essentially turns the switch on and off. The difference is that instead of a using a magnetic-field sensor, it uses a light-field sensor.

Inside the distributor housing, a light-sensing receptor is mounted directly across from a small LED that produces the light. The opening and closing of the shutter wheel breaks the light beam to the receptor and that produces the trigger signal for the self-contained electronic control.

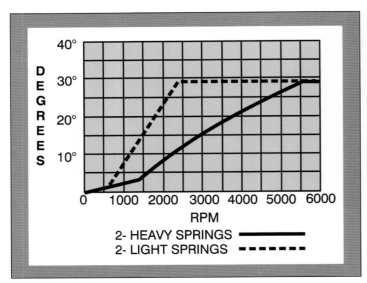

This graph shows the variety of timing curves you can achieve by simply changing the advance springs on a distributor. The spring tension controls the speed or rate that the weights move to advance the timing.

Most vacuum advance canisters use a ported vacuum source that is above the throttle plates on a carburetor. This means there is only advance when the throttle blades are open. This Edelbrock carb has a ported vacuum on the left side while the center port (manifold) and the driver-side port are plugged.

Like a Hall-effect switch, an optical trigger requires a three-wire installation: a 12-volt source for the electronic control, a ground, and a trigger wire to the negative terminal on the coil. Most optically-triggered ignitions can be used as a stand-alone distributor, or they can be used to trigger an external ignition control, such as a Mallory Hyfire ignition.

Mechanical Advance

As if the distributor doesn't have enough responsibilities, it also must match the ignition timing to the ever-changing requirements of the engine. This is an important job because an engine's timing requirements change as the load and RPM increase. Chapter 3 goes into more detail about ignition timing and the available controls. The following briefly covers the distributor's timing advance mechanism.

At idle, a spark occurs on a piston's compression stroke a few degrees

Moroso offers an adjustable vacuum canister for GM's HEI, internal-coil distributor. An adjustment screw inside the canister allows you to set the amount of advance.

Rotors handle a lot of heat in a confined area. For performance and racing applications, look for a rotor with a screw-down tip for added durability.

before it reaches top dead center (TDC). At this point, the air/fuel mixture is ignited, beginning the combustion process. The act of combustion, based on time, generally remains a constant, so when the piston travels at a much higher speed the initiation of the combustion process must occur sooner. Therefore the spark must be advanced in the compression stroke

to obtain the best combustion and results on the power stroke.

To meet these demands, distributors are equipped with an advance mechanism that operates through centrifugal force.

This mechanical advance assembly is made up of two weights that are pushed out by the spinning force of the distributor. Springs are attached

Electronic Mechanical Advance

In this modern, digital world, we sometimes find ourselves still swapping springs and bushings to control the centrifugal advance of distributors. Not any more, as Crane and MSD offer digital alternatives.

Both companies have distributors that use a microprocessor to control the timing. You adjust or choose a timing curve through little rotary dials on the side or inside of the housing. Even the vacuum advance is controlled through the electronics. You'll never have to adjust springs and weights again!

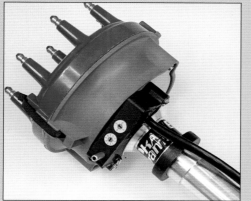

Crane developed a distributor that uses electronics instead of weights and springs for an advance. Two rotary dials allow you to set the advance, plus there's also a port for vacuum advance. One of their ignition controls is required to use this distributor.

MSD offers the E-Curve, a distributor with an electronic advance. These distributors are a stand-alone unit, meaning they do not require an ignition control box. It has numerous timing curves and vacuum advances, plus a built-in rev limiter. It's perfect for restored cars to fire up the spark and protect the engine from over-rev damage from a missed shift.

to the weights to control the rate at which they extend. The weights are mounted on an advance plate, and typically a nylon pad (or something similar) allows the weights to slide for smooth timing transitions. A stop bushing of some type controls the total amount of advance. It moves forward because it is attached to the trigger assembly of the distributor.

By swapping springs with different tension, you can alter how quickly the timing advances. A spring with less tension lets the weight spin out easier to advance the timing quickly.

The mechanical advance is an important element in tuning your engine. A slow advance can hinder performance, while too much advance can cause pre-ignition resulting in a loss of power or even engine damage. This is why it is important to check the timing at idle and at higher RPM so you know where the total advance is set.

Many companies offer advance kits consisting of different weights

MSD's Cap-A-Dapt kits give you the ability to install a larger distributor cap and rotor, if you have the clearance. They have kits available for most of their applications, like this huge Pro-Cap version that is installed on a front-drive distributor.

and springs to fit a variety of distributors so you can dial in an advance curve to match your engine's needs.

Vacuum Advance

Vacuum-advance canisters were used primarily to increase the engine's fuel economy. The canister provides a way to advance the ignition timing during moderate and part-throttle conditions. This is when the load on the engine is low and vacuum is high. The canister has a diaphragm with a mechanical link connected to the pickup plate in the distributor. When vacuum is applied, the pickup plate is pulled, the trigger signal is created, and the timing is advanced. Vacuum drops when the engine is accelerated, so the advance turns off to prevent detonation.

In most cases, the vacuum source for an advance canister is located above the carburetor's throttle plates. The result is called ported vacuum. Manifold vacuum occurs when an inlet is connected directly to the intake manifold.

The difference is that manifold vacuum is constant. The ported source provides vacuum only when the throttle blades are open, which is the way most vacuum advance systems are connected.

The amount of advance that occurs varies, but it generally ranges from 10 to 15 degrees. Some companies offer an adjustable vacuum-advance canister that lets you set the exact amount of vacuum advance that your engine requires.

Caps and Rotors

The distributor cap and rotor are part of the secondary side of the ignition, which means they receive the high voltage from the coil. These components are important to performance and should be inspected and replaced periodically to remain trouble-free. How often really depends on how frequently you drive your car and even where you live.

A lot of humidity and changes in temperature cause corrosion to occur in the cap. When an engine is run, the air within the cap heats up and then cools again when the engine is shut off, causing condensation. This, in turn, causes the brass terminals of the cap to corrode. Racers and other performance enthusiasts sometimes drill a few holes in the cap to help vent the air.

The rotor and cap on a race engine should be inspected as part of routine maintenance between events. Check inside the cap for signs of carbon tracking; this is the sign of spark scatter. Carbon tracking appears as a small jagged line that looks as if someone drew it with a pencil.

Check the tightness of the rotor screws and inspect the rotor tip for

In high-humidity regions, drilling a few holes in the distributor cap helps vent the ozone gases that can build up inside smaller distributor caps. The holes should be beneath the rotor skirt and about 3/8 inch in diameter. This is supplied predrilled from MSD.

signs of pitting or wear, especially on the end. High-output ignitions can put a lot of heat across the rotor tip, so keep an eye on it. Also, sparks like to have a nice sharp edge to cross over to the plug wire terminal, so if the rotor tip is rounded from wear, it's time replace it.

Don't scrimp on an OEM-type rotor if a better aftermarket one is available for your application. Stock parts are made from easy-to-break plastic and most only have the tip pressed in place. Look for a rotor with a tip that is screwed down for improved strength and durability.

Diameter Matters

A lot of electrical activity is going on inside the distributor cap. The rotor receives eight spark pulses and delivers them to eight different posts within one rotation. These sparks mix with the stagnant air inside the cap to form a gas (ozone), which can be slightly conductive. You don't want this to happen in your cap.

When choosing a distributor for a high-performance engine, try to go with the largest cap and rotor that will fit your application. This is less important for mild street applications, as these engines are at moderate throttle and cruising with low load most of the time. A racecar is a different matter, however, so the bigger the cap the better.

Increasing the diameter of the cap creates more room inside the cap so the terminals are spaced farther apart. This helps ensure that the spark gets to the right terminal at the correct time. Of course, some situations simply do not allow for a large distributor cap. When this is the case, the cap and rotor need to be inspected frequently, and if it's a racecar then inspection between runs is paramount.

DISTRIBUTORS AND TIMING
DIALING IN CENTRIFUGAL ADVANCE

Before choosing a distributor, you need to consider your application and what you need from a distributor. Many versions are available in the aftermarket. And what about rebuilding your own?

One of the most important features of a distributor for street cars is the centrifugal advance. When you step up to a new distributor, be sure to pick one with an adjustable mechanical advance. Having the abil-

ity to match a timing curve to your engine's needs will help make sure you're getting all the performance possible from your engine.

Choosing a Distributor

Cost is of obvious concern, and not all engines are going to require a top-end distributor. You also need to watch out for extremely inexpensive replacement distributors because you get what you pay for.

Also remember that the distributor is usually responsible for driving the engine's oil pump as well as controlling the timing. Don't be drawn in by cast-aluminum distributors that have been polished smooth so they appear to be billet aluminum. For these distributors to be priced low, some corners must be cut in the quality.

In short, do your research so you're aware of what you're buying and know the company that built it.

If you're rebuilding an engine for a muscle car that is going to be mostly stock, you may even consider keeping the original distributor. If you choose this route, make sure the

Having a plan for your engine's intended use and performance goals will lead you to the right distributor setup. Having the distributor, timing, and centrifugal advance setup for your needs is important to your engine's overall power and feel.

Do You Need Vacuum?

The vacuum advance canister that you see hanging off the side of many distributors is another form of advancing the timing, but it does not really play a performance role.

Vacuum canisters were introduced to improve economy during times of high vacuum, such as moderate cruising speeds. The advance only happens under these conditions, and once you accelerate, vacuum drops and the timing returns to the mechanical amount. You can see why they're not important to race engines.

Some engine builders have noted that a big-cubic-inch engine, such as an Oldsmobile or Pontiac 455, actually runs a little cooler on long moderate drives when it is equipped with a vacuum advance. When it comes to vacuum advance, check your engine specifications or with the engine builder for recommendations. There are too many variables; and remember that excessive advance can result in detonation.

A vacuum advance canister generally advances the timing by 10 to 15 degrees. You can also get vacuum canisters that allow you to adjust the amount of advance. Vacuum advance works as an economy boosting tool and isn't required on performance applications.

distributor is in good mechanical working condition. That is, the shaft doesn't wobble, the gear is in good condition, and the advance assembly moves freely and returns to its idle position.

Once you are confident the mechanicals are in good working order, you can decide on a trigger for the ignition and whether you want to add a high-output ignition to improve driveability. Of course, an electronic replacement kit (such as one from Pertronix, Crane, or Mallory) is a good upgrade over breaker points. If your old engine uses a little

oil or runs a touch rough at low RPM, think about installing a hotter ignition module or stepping up to a multiple-sparking ignition control. The multiple sparks really help burn rich air/fuel mixtures, and you can retain the stock distributor for appearance if you mount the control box in an inconspicuous location.

If you're putting together a moderate-performance drivetrain and plan to take advantage of this power with a heavy left foot, a new high-quality distributor should be in your future. Inaccurate triggering, poor timing advance, shaft

wobble, or slop in the gear mesh rob your engine of power. The benefits of a stout new housing with fresh bearings or bushings and a smooth mechanical advance that can be adjusted to suit your engine's needs will quickly prove themselves worth the investment.

There are more things to consider. What style of pickup seems to work best? Do you need vacuum advance for your engine? Do you have room for a large HEI-style distributor with the internal coil? What style camshaft are you running and does it require an iron, steel, or bronze (race

A Mallory Unilite distributor provides a solution for rodders with firewall clearance issues. This car, however, still required a large relief. Plan ahead for any clearance issues with your distributor. It could save you a lot of time and aggravation down the road.

If your engine block or heads have been decked, or if you're running a special block with a raised cam, you may need to shim the distributor housing or get one with an adjustable slip collar. This allows you to compensate for the different height of the mounting surface of the intake manifold.

No Boxes Please

Many aftermarket distributors require an external ignition box. Most of MSD's Pro-Billet distributors require a CD ignition control such as a 6AL. There are certainly performance benefits of running the external ignition, but some people prefer not to or simply don't have the real estate to mount an external ignition control.

Accel, Mallory, and MSD offer distributors that are ready to go for these situations. MSD's Ready-to-Run distributors have an inductive ignition module (much like a GM HEI) built into their housings to control the sparking chores. This ignition produces a high-powered spark but does not deliver multiple sparks as their other ignitions do. These distributors are a good choice for street rods that lack room for mounting extra parts, plus they offer a clean installation. The Ready-to-Run distributor from MSD has three wires versus the two wires of their standard distributors.

Mallory offers a variety of distributors that are stand-alone models as well as several with smaller housings that fit in tight engine compartments. You can even get new points distributors that drop right in and fire the coil with improved advance assemblies and features.

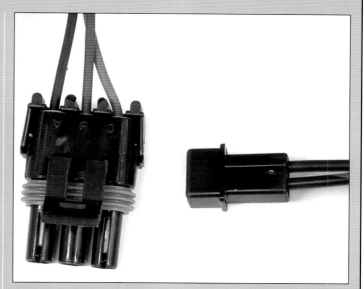

The two-pin magnetic pickup connector on the right is from an MSD distributor and requires an ignition box such as their 6A series. The connector to the left is an MSD Ready-to-Run distributor, which does not require an external box. The three wires connect to ground, coil positive, and coil negative.

only) distributor gear? Has your engine been decked or machined, or is it a tall-deck block that requires a special housing? How much clearance does your intake combination or firewall allow? Many street rods or midsize pony cars don't have much in the way of room, which can limit your distributor selection. The aftermarket offers a variety of models; some have small-diameter housings for these circumstances.

Timing Changes

The tricky thing about ignition timing is that one setting is just not ideal for the variety of different conditions through which an engine goes. When it comes to achieving optimum torque and horsepower throughout the entire RPM range, the ignition-timing curve is critical.

The timing that you need during cranking and at an idle is not sufficient for high-RPM operation. Conversely, ideal high-RPM timing is not going to go over well during cranking or low-speed operation. As RPM increases, the engine requires different ignition timing due to changes that occur to the air/fuel mixture entering the cylinder. The main reason is that the mixture has less time to completely combust before

FACTOR	ADVANCE TIMING FOR	RETARD TIMING FOR
Cylinder Pressure	Low	High
Vacuum	High	Low
Energy of Ignition	Low	High
Fuel Octane	High	Low
Mixture (Air/Fuel)	Rich	Lean
Temperature	Cool	Hot
Combustion Chamber Shape	Open	Compact
Spark Plug Location	Offset	Center
Combustion Turbulence	Low	High
Load	Light	Heavy

All of these statistics need to be considered when you're looking for the optimum timing setting for your application. Engine shops or manufacturers can point you in the right direction when setting the timing. Testing and tuning are the best tools you can use.

Where's the Improvement?

You just installed a new trick distributor, and after setting the timing, you head out for a test spin. The engine sounds fine but it just seems a little doggy or isn't quite what you thought it would be with the new distributor. Did you tweak the centrifugal advance to match your engine?

Most aftermarket distributors are equipped with stiff (slow-reacting) advance springs. The reason behind this thinking is to prevent detonation. If a new distributor were to be dropped in and cause an engine to rattle or, worse yet, cause damage due to detonation, it would be a bad deal for everyone involved. Having the slower, stiffer springs in place prevents that from occurring. It should also get everyone to thumb through the installation instructions to figure out how to modify the curve to match their engine's specs.

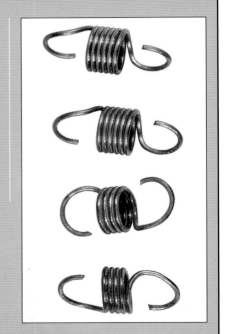

The tension of the spring used on the centrifugal advance dictates how quickly the timing advances. The two springs on the top have a thicker-gauge wire and two more coils compared to the blue springs on the bottom.

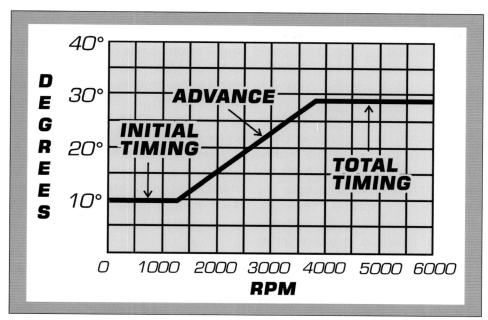

This chart shows a typical timing curve with the initial timing, the centrifugal advance, and the total timing.

the piston reaches TDC due to its increased speed.

To achieve the most force possible on the piston it is necessary to match the spark with the piston's changing speed and position before TDC. The combustion event of the air/fuel mixture remains a constant for the most part, but the change in piston speed controls when the spark must occur. At higher RPM, the piston travels through the compression stroke more quickly than at an idle; therefore, the spark must occur sooner to accomplish ideal combustion.

Many other variables also affect ignition timing. Fuel quality, com-

bustion chamber design, intake combinations, cam specifications, and more all need to be taken into consideration when setting the timing. For instance, a cam with a big profile that improves breathing efficiency at the top end needs more timing advance at low RPM. If the engine has been worked over to improve its breathing efficiency and has a higher compression ratio, less overall timing is required.

Changes in ignition timing are not limited to high-performance engines and racecars. Just about any vehicle that ever rolled off an OEM assembly line required timing changes. Before modern computer controls handled the timing chores, engineers took advantage of centrifugal force by using a mechanical advance system inside the distributor to alter the timing as RPM increased.

Yes, there hasn't been a new car with a distributor and centrifugal advance in almost two decades. Nevertheless, most of the engines being built for the street or mild strip are using this method and getting excellent results.

Definitions

Before actually setting up a distributor or checking the timing, be sure you understand these concepts.

Initial timing (sometimes called the idle timing) refers to the timing when the engine is at idle. This is the distributor's "neutral" position in the engine relative to centrifugal (mechanical) advance.

Centrifugal advance is the curve that occurs to advance the timing as RPM increases. Centrifugal (or mechanical) advance generally has two parts: the rate at which the timing advances and how far the timing advances.

Total timing is the final point that the timing is able to reach. For instance, if you have the initial timing set at 10 degrees with an advance curve limited to 24 degrees, the total timing is 34 degrees. Just how quickly this point is achieved depends on the RPM, acceleration, and rate of advance. You may have noticed that I didn't mention anything about vacuum advance involvement in setting the total timing of an engine. This is because a vacuum canister is largely a tool to gain economy and is not used in performance and racing applications. Even on street cars, the initial and total timing are always checked with the vacuum canister disconnected and the vacuum source plugged.

Centrifugal Advance

The centrifugal, or mechanical, advance assemblies consist of two weights that are pushed out by the centrifugal force of the distributor. Have you ever been on one of those traveling fair rides that spins you around, then eventually the floor drops but you stay in the same position with your body firmly planted against the wall? If not, you're missing the first-hand effect of centrifugal force.

Weights are connected to the advance plate that holds the trigger mechanism. As the weights are pushed out, the advance plate moves the pickup or pole piece opposite the rotation of the distributor. The result is that the ignition is triggered sooner.

The weights of the advance assembly have small springs that control how fast the weights are pushed out. The centrifugal force from the engine RPM has to overcome the tension of the springs. Therefore, the springs control how quickly the timing is advanced. A heavy spring requires higher RPM, resulting in a slower advance, while lightweight springs allow the centrifugal advance to occur more quickly. Generally, a quick advance rate helps most applications. Many companies (including Moroso and Mallory) offer kits with different advance weights and springs so you can dial-in a timing curve to your stock distributor.

Some aftermarket distributors also have a replaceable stop bushing that gives you the ability to limit the total amount of advance. This is an

Most aftermarket distributors have the ability to stop the advance. In the case of an MSD distributor, four stop bushings bolt in place under the advance plate. A larger diameter allows less advance.

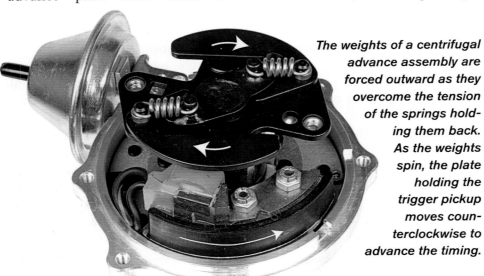

The weights of a centrifugal advance assembly are forced outward as they overcome the tension of the springs holding them back. As the weights spin, the plate holding the trigger pickup moves counterclockwise to advance the timing.

A distributor test bench allows you to spin the distributor and set up the advance before installing it in your car. Finding one, or even someone who knows how to use it is getting tough. Companies that specialize in distributors, such as Davis Unified Incorporated, take note of your engine's specs and tune an advance curve to match your needs before sending it to you. Another option is to rent some tuning time on a chassis dyno to get your distributor and power dialed in.

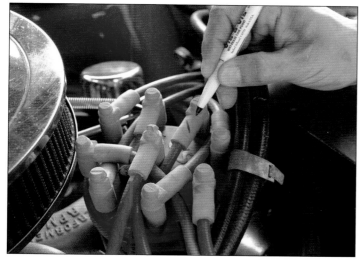

Before removing the spark plug wires and distributor cap, always mark the spark plug wires, their location, and the firing order of the engine. This saves you hassles, and possibly backfires, when re-installing them.

important feature that keeps your engine out of detonation at high RPM. An MSD distributor comes with four bushings that have different diameters to allow the advance plate to move a prescribed distance that equates to the number of degrees of timing advance. The four bushings supplied allow for 18, 21, 25, and 28 degrees of advance.

As you would expect in today's world of electronic controls, distributors are also available with electronic timing advance. Crane, Mallory, and MSD offer distributors that feature programmable, advanced electronics or have built-in rotary dials that allow you to select different timing curves. They even offer an adjustable vacuum advance. What will they think of next? Probably an app of some sort to adjust the timing!

Removal and Installation

For some reason, people never seem to want to pull the distributor out of the engine. They do have a point in that yes, the timing needs to be checked and adjusted. However, if you're replacing points or doing some maintenance on the

advance, taking the distributor out of the engine is worth the extra little bit of work, and it is actually very easy to do.

Removal from Engine

Start by removing the distributor cap. A few of the wires probably need to be pulled off, so it is a good idea to mark all of the wires and their locations. With the cap off, rotate the engine until the rotor is pointing at a fixed mark. Line it up with a bolt on the intake, straight ahead, or make a mark on the firewall. When you reinstall the distributor, the rotor

must line up at this point exactly, so it is important to have a mark that is easily identified. You can also mark the distributor housing and intake manifold. This gets the timing closer to your setting, but it isn't necessary.

Once everything is aligned and marked, loosen and remove the distributor hold-down clamp and move it out of the way. As you pull the distributor out, the rotor turns slightly because of the helical gear that meshes to the cam gear.

Reinstallation

Before you reinstall the distributor, make sure the gasket or O-ring is in place on the housing. If the distributor is clean, it's a good idea to put some oil or grease on the distributor gear (this is absolutely required when installing a new distributor or gear).

Lower the distributor into the engine and make sure the rotor is in the vicinity of the mark you made. Remember, the helical gear does not allow the rotor tip to align until the distributor is fully seated. If the distributor just won't fully seat or align, chances are the oil pump shaft needs to be rotated.

Turn the engine over until the rotor is facing an easy-to-align-to mark. This could be something on the firewall, a bolt on the intake, or simply a point straight ahead. Note that the distributor rotates a little due to the helical cut of the gears when you lift it out. Take that into consideration when you're reinstalling it.

On most Fords you can simply wiggle the shaft a little and get it to align or you may need to use a socket (be sure to tape it to an extension so it doesn't drop into the engine) to turn the oil pump shaft.

On Chevrolet engines, you may need to use a long, flat-blade screwdriver to turn the oil pump shaft a little and try again. The distributor drops into position.

Once the distributor is in place with the rotor aligned, install the hold-down clamp and distributor cap. Then start the engine and adjust the timing.

Brand-New Distributor

Removing and installing a distributor from a running engine is one thing, as you already have marks and indications of where the distributor needs to be positioned. Installing the distributor in a new engine or one that has never been turned over takes a little more work, but is easy to accomplish.

To start, you need to find TDC on the number-1 cylinder. If the valve cover is off, you can watch the valves as you rotate the crankshaft. Both valves are closed (during the combustion event) when the mark on the balancer aligns with the TDC mark of the timing indicator. If the valve covers are sealed, you can remove the number-1 spark plug and place your finger over the spark plug hole while rotating the engine. As the piston comes up on the compression stroke you will feel the air being pushed around your finger as the timing mark aligns with the indicator to show TDC.

With the crankshaft in the correct position, prepare the distributor with a new seal by coating the gear with the supplied break-in lube (this

is even more important on new camshafts). If your new distributor did not come with any break-in lube, stop the installation and make a run to your speed shop. Break-in lube has specific properties and lubrication capacities to help these gears mesh together during the initial start up of the engine.

On a fresh installation, you have the opportunity to position the number-1 cylinder at any of the distributor cap terminals. (That is, as long as you haven't made your plug wires a custom length and it won't reach.) Before engaging the distributor to the oil pump shaft or cam gear, simply rotate the shaft to move the rotor tip to where you want the number-1 spark plug wire to connect.

Lower the distributor into place but keep in mind that you may have to move the oil pump shaft slightly to align properly with the distributor shaft. Once aligned, the distributor slides down to the block-mating surface. Note that the rotor turns slightly because of the helically cut gear.

Indicate the rotor position on the outside of the distributor housing with a marker. This is TDC for number-1 and gives you a reference point to position the distributor to have a little advance (or lead) to help start the engine. Remember, to advance the timing move the distributor opposite to the rotation (most Chevy engines rotate clockwise; some Fords and Pontiacs rotate counterclockwise).

Once positioned and tightened in place, install the spark plug wires following the specific firing order for your engine and connect the pickup to the coil or ignition. You'll be ready to fire up the engine and set the timing with a timing light.

Adjusting Ignition Timing

Accurately checking and adjusting the timing sounds easy enough, and it is, but there are a lot of things to take into consideration. The timing needs to be checked at idle and as you accelerate so you can see where the total timing is set.

Timing Light

A timing light has an inductive pickup that clamps to the number-1 spark plug wire. When the spark travels through the plug wire, the pickup senses it, making the strobe in the timing light flash to show the position of the timing indicator on the balancer. This is the same effect a strobe light on a dance floor has when it seems to freeze you for a fraction of a second. On the engine it occurs much faster.

As with most tools, there are several versions of timing lights available, and they can range from fairly cheap to upward of a couple hundred dollars. If you're shopping for a light, ask yourself what you want to accomplish and how much you can spend. If you're only going to occasionally set the timing on your street machine you may not need a double-throw-down digital dial-back timing light with a triple chrome housing and carbon-fiber carrying case. However, if your engine strives for dead-nuts-accurate timing within a degree, stepping up to a better-quality light could be beneficial.

The most important quality in a timing light is accuracy. This can be tough to pinpoint. The only real way to test a light's accuracy is with advanced electronic equipment. You could compare your light with a friend's light and another light, but which one is correct? The main thing

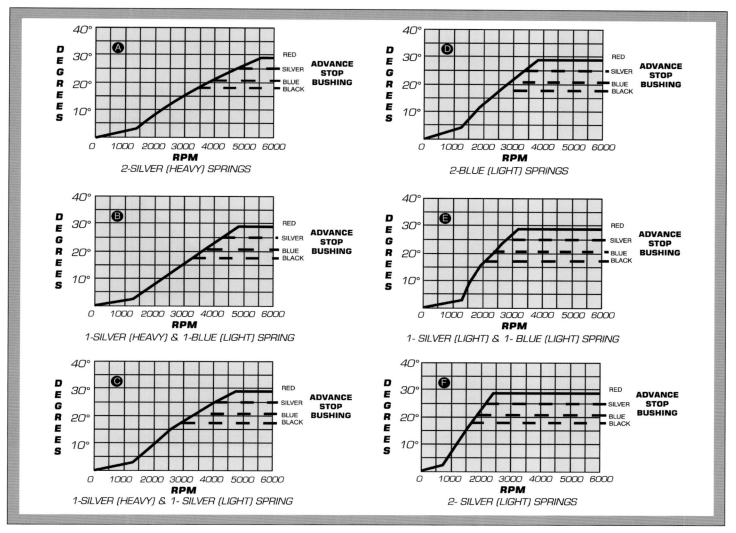

These charts illustrate the number of different curves you can "program" into a mechanical advance. Simply swap three sets of advance springs and four stop bushings supplied with an MSD distributor to make changes.

Finding the timing indicators can sometimes be a hassle. Having a degreed balancer or a timing tape and a clean, easy-to-view indicator are important. A good timing light is critical when you're tuning your ignition timing.

Dial-Up Total Timing

Dial-back timing lights are helpful in checking the centrifugal advance and total timing, especially if your engine doesn't have a degreed balancer. These lights have buttons or a dial on the back of the housing that is marked off incrementally in degrees.

After checking and setting the initial timing, you can position this dial to your desired total timing. If you're shooting for 40 degrees of total timing by 3,000 rpm, you simply set the dial on 40 degrees and begin to rev up the engine. At first, you don't see the indicator on the balancer, because it is 40 degrees before top dead center (BTDC). As the RPM increases, the indicator on the balancer becomes visible.

If everything is set up properly, the indicator aligns with the zero mark when your timing reaches 40 degrees. This is a nice feature since you don't need a degreed balancer or timing tape.

This digital dial-back distributor allows you to punch in a total timing goal (20 degrees in this example). When the centrifugal advance is completely in, the timing mark should align with zero. The term dial-back comes from the original design of this style of light but had a good old rotary dial for adjustments.

is to stick with a light that provides repeatable results.

Next to accuracy, one of the most important features is the brightness of the strobe. You need something with a very bright strobe that is easy to read even in bright daylight. Sometimes it's tough to locate the timing pointer on an engine, so having a light that can easily brighten up the indicator and the degree marks makes timing tuning easier.

Another thing to look for is a timing light with a metal inductive pickup that clamps to the spark plug wire. A low-quality plastic pickup inevitably meets an exhaust header and you're stuck with a useless inductive blob. Metal pickups are hard to find, so at least make sure the pickup is made of a good-quality plastic and that it clamps or locks in place.

It is important to always use the same light on your car. Never use one light at home or on the dyno and then swap to a different light at the track. It is also important to use the same ignition system at the engine

dyno and the track, as timing variances can occur among ignition controls as well. Being consistent in the pits with the way you tune up and work on your car will lead to consistent performance on the track.

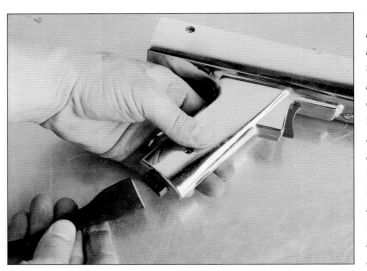

Timing lights with removable leads lend themselves to tidy storage. More important, if they ever get caught in the fan, you won't be out an entire light. The damage will be limited to the harness (and not the radiator), which can be replaced for a few bucks.

Indicators and Degrees

You can have the brightest, most accurate timing light available, but if you don't have a clear timing mark on the balancer or pointer, it's not going to do you any good. A factory-timing pointer is designed to be adequate at best, and it just wasn't intended for precise tuning capabilities. Most are flimsy, stamped pieces with hard-to-read numbers or simple notches. Stock balancers have a timing line stamped at the TDC point for the number-1 cylinder, so there's not

A self-powered timing light is helpful in applications where the battery has been relocated to the trunk, such as on drag cars or street rods. They use internal batteries, so there are no wires to connect to power and ground. These are also ideal for race engines with magnetos because they don't have a battery to power the light.

Having a good-quality distributor hold-down clamp is often overlooked and could become a necessity when running a high-pressure oil pump combined with thicker oil due to the added forces working against the shaft. Many clamps are thick, flex-free steel and have machined tips that grip the sleeve of the distributor. Some of these beefy models may not work with stock-style cast housings, so be sure to consult the manufacturer.

Timing Tips

With your trusty timing light in hand, you're ready to get the distributor settled in place. Remember that the engine is going to be running and you'll even be revving the engine; always make sure to take the necessary safety precautions.

Connect the inductive pickup to the number-1 plug wire. Make sure the wiring of the timing light does not get moved or pulled near moving components.

If you are adjusting the distributor with the engine running, try to grab the base of the distributor to make adjustments. If you have a high-output ignition providing the fire, this makes a good ground source for the spark to run to. Get a buddy to rotate the distributor while you watch the timing.

After getting the initial timing positioned, tighten the distributor's hold-down clamp, and then check the total timing by revving the engine to about 3,000 rpm. You'll see the timing mark advance. If the advance is not what you were thinking your total should be, you may need to adjust the centrifugal advance.

Some timing light inductive pickups are directional and must be connected in a certain way to get a correct reading.

The timing indicators on this old Pontiac are pretty clear up to 16 degrees, but it won't be of much help setting up the mechanical advance. The degreed balancer helps, or a dial-back timing light would be better.

A numbered timing decal can be applied to the balancer to help set the timing more accurately. Be sure to clean off any grease or grime so the tape sticks well. Make sure to match the decal to the diameter of the balancer or the degree increments will be off.

much of a chance to check the total advance. This combination doesn't make for the most accurate way to set the ignition timing.

Most aftermarket balancers come with timing degrees marked off through 90 degrees BTDC. Some are fully degreed so you can view the timing of different cylinders. If you have stock components, you can add a timing tape to the balancer to help check the total timing. (This is a perfect example of when a dial-back timing light is nice.) These tapes are matched to balancers with different diameters and feature degreed increments to help with the timing.

Proper Gears and Mesh

How the distributor is driven is important to its accuracy and longevity. Camshafts are made of different blends of metals and materials, so the distributor gear must be made of compatible metallurgical materials. Generally, the distributor gear is made of a slightly softer metal so if

there is a failure, the distributor gear takes the brunt of the destruction, simply because it is less expensive and easier to replace.

The gear that is right for your engine is dependent on the camshaft. It is best to contact the cam manufacturer for a recommendation, but here are some general tips.

An iron gear, supplied with most distributors, is the choice for flat-tappet camshafts and is the most common mild replacement cam. A bronze gear, most common in racing and high-performance engines, is an option if you have a roller camshaft.

Throughout the 1990s, hydraulic roller camshafts were used in numerous OEM engines and they are still lifting the valves in many of their crate engines. Most of these camshafts require a special steel distributor gear. A prime example is the Ford 302 of the late 1980s through the mid-1990s that comes with a hydraulic roller cam and therefore requires a steel gear.

With the degrees marked off on the balancer, all you need is a solid pointer to read the timing. Aftermarket versions are available or you can simply fabricate one out of steel wire. Just make sure it is mounted solidly and does not move.

EFI Timing

On early-model cars with distributors and electronic fuel injection, such as the 5.0-liter Mustangs, the distributor doesn't have a centrifugal advance curve. Timing chores are handled by the ECU, and the distributor is simply locked out. You can still watch the timing change by revving the engine through the RPM range while using a timing light.

To check the timing on a Ford car equipped with a TFI (thick film integrated) ignition module, you need to find the "spout" connector. This is generally in the engine compartment near the distributor or on the passenger's-side wheel well. With the engine running, disconnect the connector to put the car in open-loop mode, which sets the timing at the initial point for adjustment. GM cars can be checked in a manner similar to this, as there is a single brown-and-white wire that needs to be disconnected. Once the initial timing is adjusted, turn the engine off, reconnect the wiring, and go for a test drive.

The main benefit of moving to an aftermarket distributor on a late-model EFI car is for its strength and fresh tolerances. This Mallory distributor is a replacement for Ford TFI ignition modules. The billet housing is stronger than the original cast version, plus it is supplied with a better-quality cap with retainer.

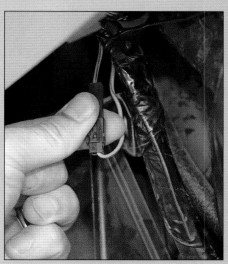

On engines with distributors that were electronically controlled (mid-1980s to early 1990s), there is a single wire connector that must be disconnected to accurately set the timing. Disconnecting this connector bypasses the timing input from the ECU so all that shows is initial timing. The Ford "spout" connector from a TFI ignition module was typically under the hood; GM had some under the passenger's side of the dash as well as under the hood.

Gear material depends on the camshaft used. Different core materials are used in a variety of cam applications, and you need to make sure you have the correct distributor gear to match the camshaft. Most distributors are supplied with iron gears, which may not be compatible with many hydraulic roller cams. Most hydraulic rollers require a steel, bronze, or composite gear. Bronze gears are not terribly durable for street use and are used mostly by racers, and the composite gears are somewhat pricey, about twice the cost of the alternatives. The most important thing is to match the gear that is appropriate for the composition of your cam. Check with the cam manufacturer to make sure that your cam and distributor are compatible.

Comp Cams offers a completely different product: a composite gear. That's right, their gear is made from Carbon Ultra-Poly. It can replace steel or even bronze gears.

If the gears are not meshing properly, the timing is not accurate. This is more of a concern on high-end race engines. To compensate, some race teams may run oversized gears from + .003 to .015 inch for Chevrolet applications in an effort to tighten the gear mesh.

PERFORMANCE IGNITION CONTROLS
CHOOSING AN IGNITION FOR YOUR ENGINE

The ignition control (spark box or just plain "box") is the foundation for many aftermarket ignition systems. That is, if you choose to go with an external CD ignition control. For mild cruisers and daily drivers many people stick with a GM HEI or other inductive-based distributor. In most cases, that means less wiring and few parts under the hood, and there's nothing wrong with keeping things simple.

Just as when you're building a car, you need to have a plan. Even a loose plan will do. We all know that project car plans can change on a whim, but I'm not talking about wheels or paint colors. You need an idea of what you want to do with the vehicle. Is it a cruiser, dirt track car, or drag car that will get nitrous? If you plan on the engine producing about 350 hp, you know you don't need to spend the extra money for a set of race-prepped axles, a carbon fiber driveshaft, or an MSD Programmable Digital-7 Ignition Control and crank trigger. That would just be overkill.

Actually, the ignition is one area where going a little overboard does not have much of an adverse effect on your engine's performance. It's not quite the same effect as having too much cam lift or an oversized carb. In fact, in most cases the engine doesn't require the full potential of the ignition's output. At moderate throttle, even on a mild street engine, it could take fewer than 15,000 volts (sometimes less) to light the fuel mixture.

The point here is that if you don't know what you're looking for in an ignition, you can easily be steered into overkill. Even worse is to not have enough fire to ignite the fuel mixture, resulting in poor performance. The ideal ignition system should be somewhere between just right and a little over the top, while being within your budget.

A lot of different options are available to consider when you're selecting an ignition control for your engine. Would your engine benefit from a capacitive discharge multiple-sparking ignition? Would a rev limiter be a good idea, or is the ignition compatible with your existing distributor?

Inductive System

An inductive ignition system is used to fire the majority of stock and OEM engines. A factory inductive ignition system gets the job of creating combustion in the cylinder in an adequate fashion. There are certainly steps you can take to improve an inductive ignition's output.

An inductive system relies on the coil to carry the brunt of the system's work. The coil is responsible for taking in battery voltage (12 to 14 volts) and stepping it up to thousands of volts. It then creates a spark that is capable of jumping the gap of the spark plug to ignite the air/fuel mixture. To accomplish this, the coil is made up of two series of windings, the primary and secondary. The coil also has an iron core to strengthen the magnetic field that is created as the battery current flows through the primary windings.

Inductive ignitions serve their purpose well in many applications thanks to their long-duration spark. This can be a benefit on some engine combinations when considering engine RPM, compression, and other factors.

The biggest challenge of the inductive ignition design is the buildup and storage of voltage.

Chrysler offered three versions of ignition modules to increase the spark output of the OEM inductive-based ignition. This chrome model was recommended for increased performance through 8,000 rpm.

ICE Ignition

ICE Ignition takes a different approach to increasing the performance of an ignition. This company capitalizes on the long-duration spark of an inductive ignition design rather than using a capacitive discharge system.

ICE incorporates advanced digital circuitry to boost the voltage supply to the coil through high RPM, as well as controlling the dwell. This produces a spark with a long duration of 24 to 36 degrees of crankshaft rotation. Together, the system ensures high output through redline RPM.

These systems are offered as boosters that wire in with the factory ignition or as standalone systems complemented by the matched coil and distributor. Systems are available for applications from street performance to full racing with programmable options and features including RPM limiters and timing maps.

The advanced inductive technology from ICE Ignition delivers a powerful spark output coupled with long duration across the plug gap. The ignition is complemented with a matching inductive coil.

Electromotive Inc.

Electromotive also takes advantage of an inductive ignition's long-spark duration, but it makes up for the short coil dwell time by replacing the distributor. By incorporating one coil for every two cylinders, each coil has plenty of time to charge to full capacity. In fact, the time available to recharge each coil goes up four times on an eight-cylinder engine since it does not have to fire every spark plug.

The XDi distributorless Electromotive ignition is an inductive system that uses multiple coil packs. Because each coil only fires twice throughout an engine's complete firing cycle, each coil has more time to charge to full capacity.

It takes a certain amount of time (called dwell or coil saturation) for the coil to transform the lower battery voltage to the higher voltage required to jump the spark plug gap. This works just fine at lower RPM, but what happens as RPM increases? There may not be enough time for the coil to transform the battery voltage between firings. This can create a low-voltage spark output that may not be powerful enough to ignite the air/fuel mixture in the cylinder and that can result in a misfire and loss of power.

That isn't to say that distributor-triggered inductive ignition systems don't have their place in the performance world. In fact, with advances in high-current circuit controls and digital management, you may see more high-output inductive ignitions in the future. Several companies, including Australian-based ICE Ignition, offer a variety of inductive-based ignition controls with improved technology and output.

Capacitive Discharge System

CD ignition controls have been the mainstay of performance ignition systems since the mid-1970s. Their biggest advantage is the ability to produce full-power sparks throughout the engine's entire RPM range with no fear of a weak spark at the top end. This is because a CD ignition draws its voltage supply directly from the battery and uses a custom-wound

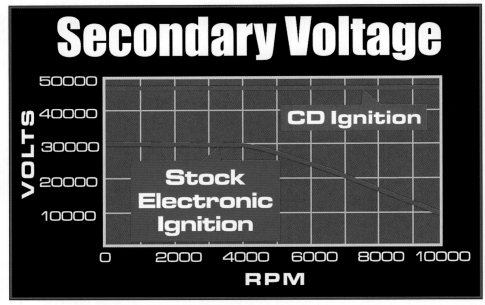

This graph illustrates the difference between the secondary voltage of an inductive ignition and a capacitive discharge ignition control. As RPM increases, the inductive output eventually falls due to the lack of time between firings. The CD ignition is always at full output power.

This is the capacitor of an MSD 6-Series Ignition (left). Next to it is the transformer that receives power directly from the battery and increases it to nearly 500 volts. The capacitor stores this voltage until the ignition is triggered, at which point all of the voltage is delivered to the coil.

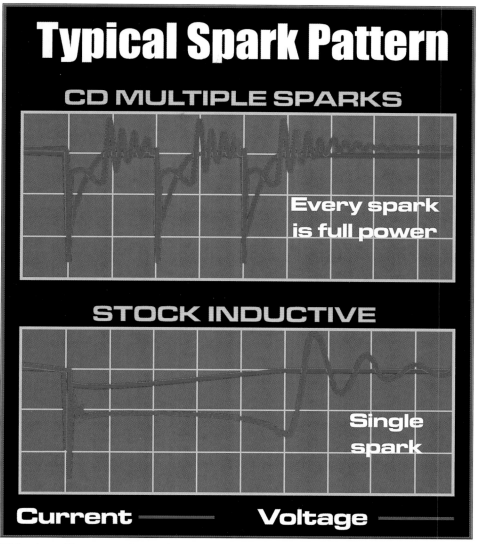

This chart illustrates the multi-sparking capabilities of most capacitive discharge ignition controls. Each spark is at full output power and the series of sparks generally lasts for 20 degrees of crankshaft rotation.

transformer to increase the voltage to 500 volts or more.

This voltage is stored at full strength and is at the ready in the ignition's capacitor. Once the ignition receives a trigger signal, all of this voltage is dumped into the coil where it is transformed to the high voltage that is required at the spark plug gap. Depending on the coil being used, the voltage could reach 30,000 to 45,000 (or more) volts.

A capacitive discharge ignition delivers the high voltage to the spark plug that is required to ionize, or create a bridge across the plug gap over which the spark energy flows. The downside of a CD ignition is that the spark has a very short duration.

At lower RPM, this could present a problem, but engineers found a solution by firing the plug multiple times in the same cycle. This is the multiple-spark, multi-strike, or second strike discharge so popular in ads and magazine articles. Most CD igni-

tions create multiple sparks when the engine is below 3,000 to 3,300 rpm. As RPM drops, the number of sparks that occur increases because there is more time to fire the plug. At an idle maybe five or six sparks occur, but only two occur at 2,700 rpm. Even with its shorter duration, a single CD spark has no trouble igniting the air/fuel mixture at engine speeds over 3,300 rpm. Remember, we're talking about cycles that occur within milliseconds!

Many people look at CD ignitions as race-only options, but that is not the case. In fact, a lot of these ignitions are legal to install on engines with pollution control; some are even legal to install on cars equipped with onboard diagnostics (OBD-II, for example). Most ignition controls are nearly universal in their application, as they can be installed on almost anything with a distributor. Of course, distributors haven't been used on newer vehicles for nearly 20

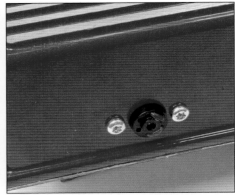

The MSD 6AL is one of the most popular CD ignitions. Most ignition companies offer a 6-series as a general all-purpose street/track ignition. It features an adjustable rev limiter and can be used on four-, six-, or eight-cylinder engines with a distributor. This is the classic design, as the 6AL went through a revision resulting in a digital design.

Behind this little cover are two loops of wire. By cutting one or both loops, you program the rev limiter to realize that it is installed on a four- or six-cylinder engine. The spark-output side of the ignition doesn't care what even-fire engine it is on, but the rev limiter circuit needs to know the cylinder count. Manufacturers use dials or cylinder loops in most cases.

years, but ignitions and coils are also available for these distributorless systems (see Chapter 8).

The series of full-power sparks that most CD ignitions produce creates more heat in the cylinder, resulting in improved combustion of the air/fuel mixture. In most cases, the benefits include improved idle, quick starts, crisp throttle response, and improved high-RPM performance. If you have an engine that burns a little oil, runs a touch on the rich side, a multiple-sparking ignition (CD or inductive) could help overcome these performance issues. That is, until they can be remedied correctly.

Keep in mind that multiple-sparking ignitions are not just for high-performance racecars. They offer a lot of great drivability benefits, such as quick starts, smooth idle, great throttle response, and top-end RPM. Another important fact is that many units even carry CARB (Cali-

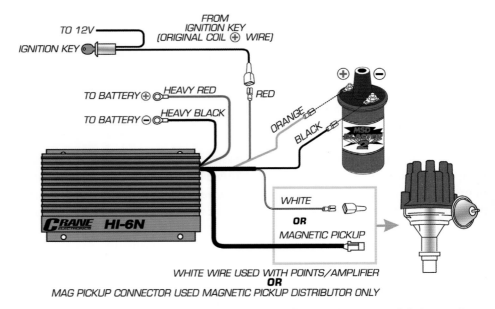

This diagram shows how easy it is to wire in a CD ignition control. It has only four wires to connect, plus the battery supply wires. Remember, these can be installed on most any engine equipped with a distributor and a 12-volt negative-ground system.

fornia Air Resources Board) approval numbers, meaning that they're legal to install on vehicles in all 50 states. Mind you, this depends on the year

of the vehicle and the model of ignition. The point is that by achieving better combustion resulting from high power and multiple sparks, an ignition control can benefit everything from a daily grocery-getter to a weekend bracket racer.

Almost any engine that is equipped with a distributor and a 12-volt, negative-ground electrical system can accept a CD ignition. A few import vehicles actually had CD systems installed from the factory; these do not accept an aftermarket CD system. Except for a handful of examples, almost every four-, six-, and eight-cylinder engine is a candidate for improved spark power.

As long as there's a distributor and a single coil, an ignition control can be added regardless of whether it's on a 1.8-liter Honda, an inline six-cylinder truck, or an LT-1 Impala SS with the distributor mounted behind the water pump. Most ignition controls are nearly universal, and if you can get to the trigger wire(s) and the coil terminals, you can install one. A CD ignition control has two power-source wires that supply the battery voltage and ground, one wire to turn the unit on and off, a coil positive wire, a coil negative wire, and a trigger input wire. Usually, a trigger input accepts a signal from points or an amplifier and another connector with two wires for a magnetic pickup. You either use the points wire or the magnetic pickup wires, but never both at the same time.

Points Plus CD Ignition

A variety of electronic conversions are available for factory-style distributors with breaker points, but other options also exist. As long as the distributor is in good mechanical condition, why not install a CD ignition to the system? Think about it: Not only do you receive the benefits of the ignition's multiple sparks and high voltage, but the points last

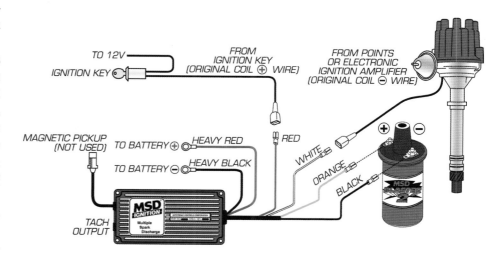

This is how easy it is to connect an MSD 6A or similar CD ignition control to a distributor with points. Benefits include better performance (due to the higher voltage sparks), longer points life, and a backup ignition. If you were to ever experience problems with the ignition, you can easily bypass it and use the points to get home.

much longer and don't require much (if any) maintenance.

A CD ignition doesn't cost much more than many electronic points replacement kits. The benefits are twofold if you don't mind mounting the control box and dealing with a few more wires. When a CD ignition, such as a 6-Series model, is wired to a points system, the points are only responsible for triggering the ignition. The transformer in the ignition increases the voltage and stores it in its own capacitor. When the points trigger the box, all of this voltage is delivered directly to the coil, where the voltage is increased even further and sent to the spark plugs.

You can see the performance improvements, but another benefit is that the points last much longer. Without a CD, the flow across the gap is 3 or 4 amps when the points are open. In addition to the mechanical side of the operation, this is the primary cause of points wear. With the CD ignition installed, the breaker points are used

only to trigger the unit to fire, so less than .3 amp bridges the gap.

RPM Limiters

An RPM limiter is cheap insurance that can save your engine and save you a lot of money in case of a missed shift, driveline failure, or other issue that may send the engine RPM through the roof. As you invest more time, effort, and money into your engine, you may start to realize its importance.

An RPM limiter is made up of a circuit that "watches" the RPM of the engine. You set the limit for your engine with an RPM module or through a switch on the ignition. When the engine reaches this RPM value, the rev-limiting circuits drop the sparks to different cylinders in order to hold the RPM at the desired limit. Even if the throttle is wide open, the goal of the RPM limiter is to never let the engine exceed the set RPM point.

Tachometer Considerations

It's important to note that when you connect the primary coil wires, they should be the only wires connected to the coil terminals. Don't try to connect your tach to the coil's negative terminal, because once the CD ignition is in place, up to 500 volts are on the coil's primary side, and tachometers don't like 500 volts.

Use care not to touch these terminals when the engine is cranking or running because you won't like the increased voltage! Also, be sure not to connect any test equipment such as test lights or dwell meters to the coil. You run the risk of damage to your testers and even more serious damage to yourself.

If you have an aftermarket tachometer that was connected to the negative terminal of the coil, don't hook it up. All of the CD ignitions have a tach output terminal that produces a common 12-volt square wave signal that should trigger the tach. On certain low-cost bargain-type tachs you may have some trouble. Again, this generally should not give you a problem. However, if your tach has trouble reading the CD ignition's tach signal, you may need a tach adapter to fix the problem; these are available from the ignition manufacturer.

Tach or Stalling Troubles

With so many applications, you are bound to run into cars or engines that surprise you and the ignition companies. For instance, after installing a CD ignition on your Toyota, it starts and runs rough, then stalls. Maybe the tachometer on your 5.0-liter Mustang reads erratically.

Chances are that most of these ignition companies have run into the problem you're experiencing and they know how to fix it. The most common solution is a small accessory called a tach adapter, even though it does more than simply fix the tachometer. Most of these adapters easily wire into the system and modify the trigger signal by making it stronger, so it can feed the ignition and the ECU to trigger the fuel injection. Other models can be used to work with current-triggered tachometers.

Tach adapters aren't required on the majority of installations. However, some, such as most Toyotas, do require one.

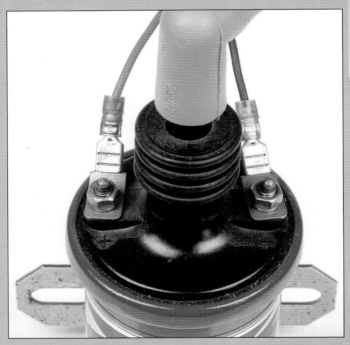

When using a CD ignition, only the orange and black wires from the ignition should be connected to the coil. Never connect a tach or test light to the coil terminals with a CD ignition installed.

A tach adapter may be needed on some applications to get the tach to trigger correctly, or even for the vehicle to run properly. In rare cases of a misfire, which is generally on foreign vehicles, these adapters boost the trigger signal and get the car fired up. Most ignition manufacturers offer them.

It Runs Great — But It Keeps Running!

You just wired in a multiple-sparking CD ignition in your 1965 Chevelle and gave the key a twist to hear the 327 fire up faster than it ever has. You're thinking that the new ignition really does make a difference. A couple snaps of the throttle and you notice a difference in how quickly the engine responds. You smile and feel satisfied that your time and money were well spent. A cruise will be the final test, but first you need to clean up a little. You turn the key off but the engine continues purring along.

This can happen on older vehicles, especially ones with external voltage regulators. The small wire that is responsible for turning the ignition control on and off is connected to a wire that is receiving feedback, most likely from the charging system dash indicator bulb. This can flow just enough voltage to keep the ignition running even after the key is turned off. In most cases, this is an easy fix.

You need to install a diode that is often supplied with many CD ignitions. This diode keeps the current flowing in one direction so it cannot feed back. The fix for some AMC engines is to use a Chrysler Dual Ballast Resistor.

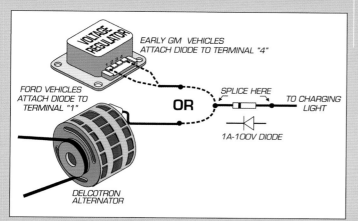

This diagram shows which wire needs a diode to prevent the engine from not shutting off.

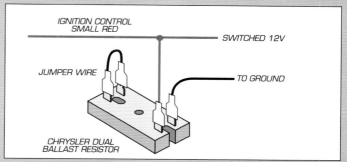

This is a dual-ballast resistor for Chrysler/AMC applications.

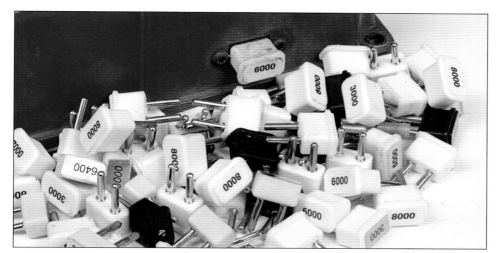

These are the infamous chips that you hear about when it comes to changing RPM limits. Inside each module is a different resistor that determines the RPM limit. They're available in 100-rpm increments from 3,000 to 12,000 rpm.

Today, most rev limit values are set through a rotary dial on the ignition or programmed via a PC but a lot of ignitions still use a module (or pill) for the rev limit value. In many circle-track racing classes, the rules impose a specific rev limit value that must be set, so if you're getting into racing, check the rule book.

Design Types

This sounds as if it is a fairly simple circuit in the ignition, but an RPM limiter has to be ready to handle various overrev situations.

First, consider accelerating at a moderate rate. As the engine

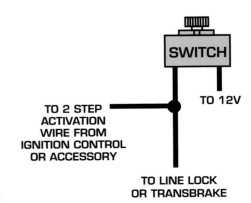

Crane, as well as most CD ignition manufacturers, uses rotary dials to adjust the rev-limit value.

Wiring a two-step rev limit is easy. The activation wire must be connected to 12 volts. By connecting it to your line-lock solenoid, or even a handheld switch, you can activate a lower RPM limit to improve your car's holeshot and your reaction time.

approaches the rev limit, say 6,000 rpm, the rev-limiting circuit senses the limit, drops the sparks to several cylinders, and easily maintains the imposed limit.

What about on a racecar? In this case, the RPM is ramping up at a rapid pace already, but all of a sudden, there's little to no load, and the result is a broken driveshaft. Hello and thank you, RPM limiter. Consider the inertia of the crankshaft (or flywheel) and the different rates of acceleration that occur in different engines. An RPM limiter needs to be able to catch the engine at the determined RPM in order to be accurate and useful to racers.

The two basic types of RPM limiters are random and sequential. As you might suspect, a random limiter drops the sparks to various cylinders in no particular order. The sequential RPM limiter uses a repeatable pattern. The sequential RPM limiter has a pattern or counts the cylinders to which it drops the spark and makes sure to fire them on the next engine cycle. This is meant to balance the cylinders and keep them from loading up with fuel.

Each circuit works well in its own way. RPM limiters seem to be getting even smoother while maintaining greater accuracy.

Two-Step Limiters

As the saying goes, most racers think that if one is good then two must be better. That thinking applies to a dual-stage RPM limiter, which is commonly referred to as a two-step. These are generally associated with high-performance ignition controls, especially those with digital control. A two-step RPM limiter offers the ability to have two independent RPM limits.

The idea behind a two-step is primarily as a drag racing accessory, as one limit can be set lower and activated on the starting line. This way, you can put the pedal to the floor and the RPM doesn't go beyond your set limit.

Most of the time, the two-step RPM limit has an activation wire that you can connect to the line lock or a trans-brake solenoid or other component that you use in the staging lights. Then when the green light comes on, the switch is deactivated and the car launches hard out of the lights. Once the two-step limit is deactivated, the over-rev limit is in effect and protects the engine from over-rev damage.

A two-step rev limit is also handy in helping the car launch consistently. It lets you concentrate on the Christmas-tree lights rather than the engine RPM.

Boost Retard

Another feature that owners of street/strip cars find useful in an ignition control is a boost retard circuit. This is obviously of use only on engines that are being force-fed air and fuel through a supercharger or turbocharger. As boost pressure increases, so do cylinder pressures. This can result in detonation, which can rob you of performance, or worse yet, damage the engine.

The MSD 6BTM (Boost Timing Master) ignition delivers the same performance and features as the 6AL, including the RPM limiter, but it also includes a boost-sensing circuit. To use the boost retard, you must route a line from the intake manifold to an inlet port on the side of the ignition so it can sense the pressure. There is also a control knob that you mount on the dash that lets you adjust the timing retard from the driver's seat. This dial is marked off from 0 to 3 degrees, and lets you adjust how many degrees of retard occur per pound of boost. As an example, if your blower produces 7 psi, with the dial set on 2 degrees, you would have a maximum of 14 degrees of retard (7 x 2 = 14).

Magnetos

Another ignition control consideration exists for engines on the ragged edge of performance. The magneto is a style of ignition that fires the spark plugs, but it's a whole different ball of wax. These aren't something you find on street cars or even drag cars (until you get into burning alcohol and nitro) or sprint cars.

One of a magneto's primary advantages is that it makes its own power, so you don't need a big, heavy 12-volt battery. A magneto is actually an inductive ignition design. It constantly generates current that is controlled through breaker points or electronic circuits to turn the current on and off. They can produce a lot of current with a long duration, plus they are mostly self-contained.

Built-In RPM and Timing Control

Most ignitions that feature a two-step rev control are digital models, and they're ideal for cars that see double duty on the street and strip. You get an engine-protecting over-rev limit, plus the consistency that a hole-shot rev limit can deliver.

The Mallory HyFire VI provides a built-in two-step RPM limiter that is easy to adjust by scrolling through the digital display that is installed on top of the housing of the ignition.

MSD's Digital-6 Plus Ignition Control provides the opportunity to set a staging/holeshot RPM limiter, plus it has a step retard option. Retard stages are a common accessory in performance ignitions. This is largely due to the popularity of nitrous-oxide injection systems.

Whenever nitrous is introduced to an engine, the timing should be retarded, because cylinder pressures go up, sometimes way up, depending on how much nitrous is introduced. If you plan to run a shot of nitrous on your street/strip car, a step retard is an important feature to have in the ignition system you choose.

Just like the staging RPM rev limit, the step feature has an activation wire that retards the timing when it is connected to a 12-volt lead. The perfect place to tie this in is by splicing it right into the nitrous solenoid wiring. That way, the timing will retard whenever the nitrous is activated.

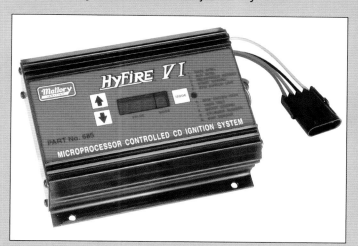

No RPM modules or rotary dials are needed to set the rev limits of the Mallory HyFire VI. This ignition features an LED screen that lets you scroll through the RPM limits and other optional settings.

Another useful option on a street/strip ignition is a step retard. MSD's Digital-6 Plus ignition provides an adjustable retard that is perfect when nitrous is being introduced to the combustion chamber. The rotary dials next to the two-step adjuster control the amount of retard.

Racing Considerations

Circle-track racing covers a broad spectrum of racing from half-mile dirt tracks to super speedways. Many rules are placed on the ignition system from mandating an HEI distributor or analog ignition to RPM limits.

Keeping Analogs

In the last couple years NASCAR moved the Sprint Cup series to EFI systems that incorporate coil-on-plug technology, effectively making the distributor and ignition boxes obsolete. The lower classes, however, still use a single coil with a distributor and ignition box.

An interesting note is that the rules allow the cars to run a completely redundant ignition system, meaning they can have two coils and two ignition boxes. Not only does this provide a backup ignition system if there were a failure (rare), but it also gives savvy builders a way to modify the ignition timing. By running a secondary pickup inside the distributor with a couple degrees of advance or retard, the driver can switch over to the second ignition system for a different timing setting. The ignition controls used in these classes must be analog based (that is, no digital microprocessors).

Crane Cams and MSD offer professional ignitions for serious circle track racing. Both ignitions are designed to deliver great power at severe racing RPM. They're also engineered to withstand the nasty environment of stock car racing. One thing both ignitions share are mandated sealed and locking connectors and a clear epoxy that must be used so tech inspectors can take a look inside the control if they deem it necessary.

These ignitions and their specific coils deliver the goods for many laps of dirt and pavement circle-track racing.

Testing Limits

A lot of circle track sanctioning bodies impose RPM limits as a way to level the playing field and keep costs under control (along with other engine regulations). Many classes require that a 7,800-rpm module be installed in the ignition's RPM limiter, or even go as far as mandating an ignition with a fixed RPM setting, such as the Crane HI-6RL Ignition. In fact, Crane offers several ignitions with fixed rev limits at 6,300, 7,400, 7,600, 7,800, 8,000, and 8,400 rpm.

However, where there are rules, racers try to find ways around them. To help the tech inspectors, and fellow racers, Crane offers a Digital Rev Limit Tester. This handy device connects inline to most racing ignitions with a Weatherpak connector. A test plug is supplied to pop onto the coil wire and then you turn the tester on and run it up to the desired RPM. The digital readout on the Tester shows the simulated engine RPM, and the RPM limiter better kick on at the designated limit or you will be busted! This is also a great tool to check the tach calibration and any other RPM-controlled devices.

Crane and MSD had to forgo their digitally controlled ignitions to adhere to NASCAR rules, resulting in the HI-6N Ignition (top) and 6HVC (bottom) series. Both ignitions feature a single-stage rev limiter and conform to other rules and regulations of the sanctioning body.

Crane's Rev Limit Tester quickly confirms the rev-limit setting during tech inspections at tracks with mandated RPM limits. The matching Weatherpak connectors plug inline for a quick look at the limit.

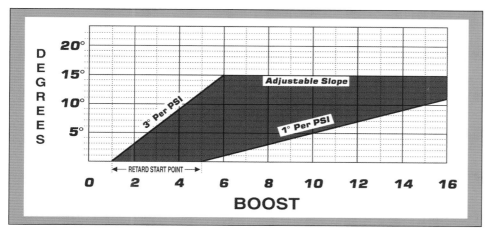

This chart illustrates timing retard in relation to boost pressure in the manifold. MSD's 6BTM lets you adjust from 0 to 3 degrees of retard per pound of boost. In addition, you can adjust the amount of boost that must occur before the retard begins.

Magnetos have their advantages, but there are reasons you don't see them on street or mild strip cars. For starters, there is the cranking RPM. To make enough current for a quality spark, a magneto must spin at a high rate, and some block-mounted starters could have trouble with the locked-out timing and engine heat. Moreover, magnetos never had the ability to incorporate timing controls, RPM limiters, and other controls that racers crave (although the MSD Pro-Mag system gives racers these opportunities). Space can be another hurdle for the magneto, as most of the generators are tall and bulky. They are also pricey. With all the improvement in battery technology, and with all the electronics that racers use these days, it's no wonder that most cars have some sort of a battery to power fuel or water pumps and acquisition controls.

MSD introduced the Pro-Mag nearly 20 years ago. They offer a Pro-Mag 12, which is a 12-amp version that is popular in sprint cars and other circle track classes. They also offer a 20-amp. The king of them all is the 44-amp Pro-Mag, used on Top Fuel and Funny Cars as well as some alcohol classes. The nitro classes use two complete 44-amp systems.

MSD magnetos use a magnetic pickup, which has allowed many teams to move to crank trigger systems and incorporate electronic timing controls. Top Fuel cars have embraced this technology and are manipulating the timing more than 15 times within a 4-second pass!

I have seen a few race teams run an MSD Pro-Mag on their turbocharged outlaw street cars. The ideal setup is to use a Power Grid controller to program timing changes, rev limits, and the details through a laptop in conjunction with the Pro Mag. Awesome power, with great control.

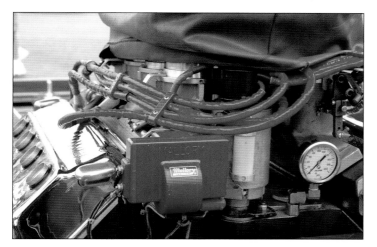

Mallory, Vertex, MSD, Don Zig, and Joe Hunt are just a few of the names you see on the sides of magnetos. Magnetos are used mostly in hard-core racing applications such as sprint cars, alcohol engines, and Top Fuel classes. This is a vintage Mallory example.

The MSD Pro-Mag 44 is used to fire the volatile mixtures that Top Fuel racing demands. These generators deliver 44 amps to their special coils with an electronic points box controlling the energy.

Programming Performance

If you plan to add a blower or nitrous, or simply want more control over your ignition timing and RPM, you should consider stepping up to a programmable ignition for the street. MSD and Mallory offer ignitions with a host of adjustments that can be made from a Windows-based PC.

These ignitions provide some terrific tuning capabilities that work great for cars that see duty on the street and track. You can map a timing curve that helps big-cam engines idle better, RPM rev limits, and timing retards including boost and other features. In several cases, these PC programmable ignitions cost less than a typical ignition with just a couple features or add-on accessories.

MSD 6AL

Face it. Computers are as much of a tool as a spark plug socket and ratchet wrench. Racers in every form of motorsports have been using laptops to program, tweak and tune, and review valuable data from the engine. It was only a matter of time for it to finally reach the street market.

If you can open, save, and file a document or photo on your computer, you should be able to work your way through without any problem. Once you get over the initial intimidation you'll really start to enjoy the benefits and versatility that computer programming provides. Changing the ignition timing with a click of your mouse rather than swapping springs or a stop bushing will spoil you.

The MSD Programmable 6AL allows you to set a two-step rev limit, set a nitrous retard, program a boost curve, and map a complete timing curve. The Pro-Data Plus software is

Mallory's FireStorm line offers standard CD ignitions as well as units that are entirely PC programmable. Everything from rev limits and timing curves to boost retards and more are set from software using a laptop.

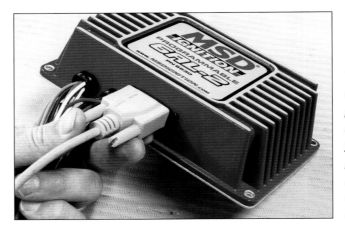

The Programmable 6AL-2 provides laptop programming for the street. Simply connect your PC to the serial port of the ignition, put away the timing light and jets, and keep your hands clean.

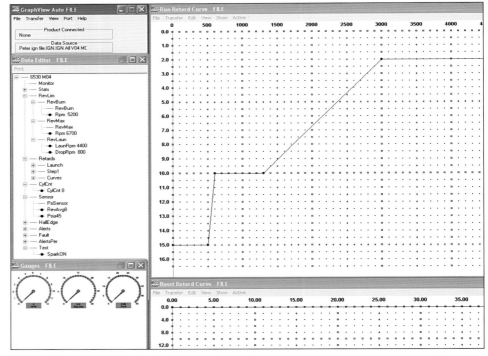

MSD's Pro-Data Plus software is designed for use with most versions of Windows. It is proven to be easy to operate and allows you to tweak and tune through timing and RPM controls.

easy to use and you can even download it at the MSD website.

The 7-Series

When you get a little more serious about performance and expect a little more impact from your ignition, you enter the 7-series zone. The 7-series ignitions from Mallory and MSD are designed for engines with higher compression, big-lift cams, high-flowing heads and intakes, big carbs or injectors, and lots of nitrous or boost pressures. In short, 7-series ignitions are meant for high-powered engines.

Most of these ignitions produce higher spark energy and increased primary voltage to the coil. To deliver more power, these ignitions also suck more current and voltage from the battery, so you have to make sure your charging system and/or battery are in great working order. In addition, most of these

ignitions are not legal for use on pollution-controlled vehicles.

Knowing when you need to step up to a 7-series ignition system is not always evident. The 6-series ignitions hold their own through so many applications, and the newest additions in recent years are even more powerful and efficient. If you already run a 6-box of some sort and continue to modify your engine to make more power, deciding when to move to a 7-series is a tough call. On naturally-aspirated engines, compression can be used as an indicator. MSD recommends a 7-series ignition on engines with more than 12:1 compression.

If your car is more of a strip/street car than street/strip car, it is in your best interest to step up to these racing ignitions. Most of them are designed for drag strip use although I have seen 7ALs on long cruises and cross-country road trips, but you need to pay strict attention to coil

selection. As comedian Jeff Foxworthy might say, "When you start to pipe in 200 additional horsepower from nitrous, you might just need a 7-series ignition."

If you have a blower that's putting more than 15 pounds of boost into the manifold, you may find yourself looking for a 7-series ignition. If your pistons are domed so high that they look like upside-down cereal bowls with valve recesses built in, you might be in need of a . . . well, you get the idea. In short, the 7-series ignitions are the most popular series when it comes to drag racing applications.

Laptop Programmables

If you find yourself in need of more RPM and timing accessories for your racing, you'll have to step up to a PC programmable ignition. MSD's Programmable Digital-7 Ignition line

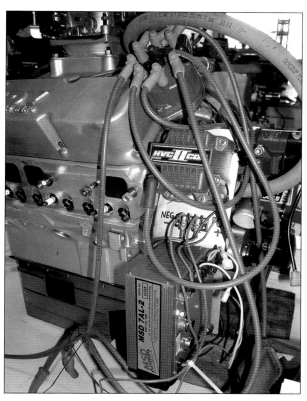

The MSD 7AL-2 has been a popular choice for drag racing engines for a long time. The ignitions deliver a higher-output spark combined with a different spark profile with extremely quick recovery characteristics. This makes them a favorite for engines with higher compression and cylinder pressure. This ignition also has a built-in two-step rev limiter that uses plug-in RPM modules for adjustment.

The MSD 7AL-3 features a three-step RPM limiter (for burnout, holeshot, and overrev protection) along with an RPM switch and four retards. These are all adjusted with plug-in modules. Digital technology provides ways to do all of this without the modules.

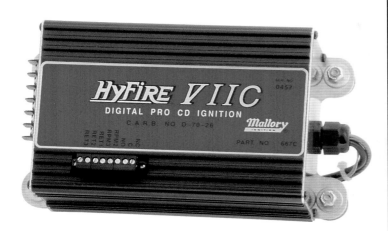

Instead of having the LED and push buttons on the ignition control, Mallory's HyFire VIIC series uses a remote digital controller connected through a removable computer harness to make adjustments. This way you don't need the ignition mounted to view the screen. (Photo Courtesy Mallory Ignition)

The MSD Programmable Digital-7 can be programmed with the optional hand-held monitor that allows you to scroll through an LCD screen to set its functions. If you plan to do some trick programming, it is best to connect your laptop and use the Pro-Data+ software to work through your programming.

or Power Grid System and the Mallory Firestorm Ignitions are the most common in the pits. These ignition controls deliver the same output as the standard 7-Series ignitions but offer a cornucopia of tuning opportunities. You can set three rev limits, set multiple retard steps, use an RPM-activated switch, map out a complete timing curve for each gear, adjust the timing of each cylinder, and much more. Programmable ignitions and their features will be discussed in detail in Chapter 7.

MSD-8

What are a tractor puller with three blown-alcohol-injected engines and a turbocharged small-block Ford that runs the quarter-mile in six seconds at more than 200 mph? They are simply over-the-top. Fortunately, there are ignition controls that climb right over the top as well, and they can deliver the spark energy that is needed.

Thinking like a racer, a 7-series ignition is seriously powerful, but an 8-series must be even better! This analog-controlled, race-only ignition creates more and more energy to maintain a powerful spark across the plug gap in the most unforgiving environment. With the advent of more powerful magnetos, the MSD-8 has a bit of a cult following and is a favorite in pulling competitions. To make the kind of power it delivers, it sucks up a lot of supply current and voltage, which makes it tough on race engines with limited battery resources.

The MSD-8 Plus has always been a favorite of tractor and truck pullers. This analog-controlled ignition produces a great amount of current and voltage energy, but it also requires a large amount of ready-reserve voltage from the battery.

COILS, WIRES AND PLUGS
TAKE A LOOK AT THE SECONDARY SIDE

Chapter 4 explained how you can improve your car's performance by adding a performance ignition control to the primary side of the ignition. Now let's take a look at the secondary, or high-voltage, side of things.

The result of an aftermarket ignition is an improved spark through CD technology and enhanced dwell control, which increases the level of the primary voltage. These ideals work well, but one thing is certain:

They cannot do it alone. These ignitions still rely on the coil. The coil takes in a low voltage with high current from an ignition (or battery) supply and transforms that electricity to a high voltage with low current to ignite whatever fuel is in the combustion chamber. It also has to accomplish these goals with great speed, efficiency, and repeatability. A lot more goes into building a coil than most people realize.

The coil wire that delivers the voltage to the distributor cap performs eight times the duty of the other plug wires. All of the plug wires have to handle thousands of volts with plenty of spark energy. Not only do they have to get the spark to the plugs, they also need to suppress the electrical interference that comes with traveling voltages. Moreover, look at their working environment! Sweltering heat, moving components, and even gale-force winds whip them around. They have to grip the spark plug to make sure the voltage makes it to the plug gap where it ionizes a path for the current to follow.

Numerous components are available to improve the performance and operation of the secondary side of the ignition system. Coils that promise huge voltage numbers or longer spark duration improve combustion. In addition, wires with the lowest resistance deliver the most current to improve combustion. Which ones are right for your ignition and application?

Coils

The coil of the ignition system is where the magic happens, as 12 volts from the battery go into the primary terminals, and thousands of volts are released through the secondary tower. Okay, we all know that magic isn't responsible for this phenomenon. It is all in the hands of electrical theory and laws of physics, even though many would still like to believe that a coil is like a magic hat. Once you see how the voltage is increased and the operation of the coil, you understand the different specifications and why certain coils can only be used for certain applications.

Inside a coil are two sets of windings: a primary set and a secondary set. The primary windings are connected to the battery and are considered the final step in the primary side of the ignition system. The primary

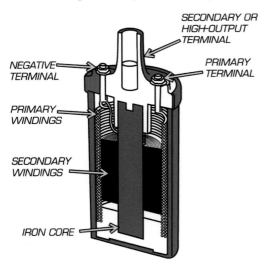

The thick primary windings are connected to the power supply of the ignition. The secondary side is made up of many more windings and is connected to the secondary tower. Engineers can vary the windings and core material for different results to match particular ignitions or applications.

windings are generally hundreds of windings and are connected between the positive and negative terminals of the coil. The secondary windings are made up of thousands of windings with a finer wire material. These windings are connected to the secondary tower of the coil and the coil primary terminal. Both sets of windings are positioned around an iron (or similar metal) core that improves the strength of the magnetic field.

When current flows through the primary windings, a magnetic field is produced. When this flow is stopped by a trigger signal, such as when the points open, the voltage is induced into the secondary windings. Due to the increased number of windings that make up the secondary side, an increase in voltage is produced. This is where a few volts are turned into the thousands of volts that fire the plug.

If you've shopped around for a performance coil or have looked at coils on different cars at shows or races, you've no doubt noticed that a lot of different coils are available. Even if you look through one ignition company's catalog, you see a variety of coils, ranging from stock replacement housings to special, race-only coils. This wide range is because many things can be altered within a coil to give it different characteristics. These differences can be an advantage to certain ignition systems, or conversely, a problem to others. Making sure that you get the right coil for your ignition and application is important to its final output.

Turns Ratio

The relationship between the primary and secondary windings is commonly referred to as the turns ratio. This is a coil specification that

you see in most catalogs and ads. Because the secondary windings consist of thousands of loops, they are compared to the primary as 100 secondary turns to every 1 primary turn for a ratio of 100:1. When 12 volts are going into the coil and the trigger breaks the flow of the current, typically a voltage spike occurs. This spike in the primary windings may reach 250 volts or more before it is induced into the secondary windings. When there is a turns ratio of 100:1, the voltage is multiplied 100 times, creating a spark output of 25,000 volts.

This is in theory, of course. Many obstacles can affect the output number, such as the heat in the coil and the loss that occurs during induction. In general, the equation works.

Engineers can alter the secondary output by modifying the turns ratio of the coil. For instance, if the same materials were used to make a coil with a 75:1 ratio, the output voltage would be 18,750 volts. If the ratio were increased to 120:1, the secondary voltage would be 30,000 volts.

All of this voltage sounds great and easy to accomplish, but there is a catch. As the voltage output is increased, the amount of current output is decreased. Likewise, as voltage is lowered, current increases. Of course, just how much these properties teeter-totter is dependent on the materials used and the makeup of the coil itself. It's a catch 22, and you must find a middle ground.

Ignition companies have to face this compromise head-on, especially when it comes to offering coils for use on street cars with inductive ignitions, for mild use with CD ignitions, and for engines that see high RPM for large amounts of time. Most entry-level aftermarket performance

Modified Honda Caps for Better Coils

On many distributor-equipped Honda and Acura engines, the coil is inside the distributor cap. To fit inside, the coil is tiny, plus it contends with engine heat while being locked under the cap. These coils work fine for thousands of miles on thousands of cars that get driven every day. However, this is a performance book, not a repair manual. Therefore, when you're looking to upgrade a Honda's ignition output, a coil upgrade is the perfect place to start.

When the coil is inside the distributor, these systems do not have a coil wire or secondary tower on the cap. How are you supposed to get the voltage from the new externally mounted coil to the rotor? You will have to use a modified cap.

MSD offers several caps for different Honda applications that are fit with a secondary coil tower. This provides a path for the high voltage of the coil to be transferred to the rotor tip and on to the spark plugs.

Honda distributor caps from MSD are fit with a secondary coil tower. The terminal is connected to a brass terminal that runs to the rotor tip. A cap like this is necessary when you move from the factory in-cap coil to an external coil with improved output.

coils deliver quality performance with a stock ignition or a mild CD ignition. For race-specific applications it becomes more important to match the coil with the ignition. Some coils are designed for the slower voltage buildup and longer duration of an inductive ignition. Others are designed to handle the high-voltage wallop that a race-only CD ignition delivers. Many things come into play.

The canister coil is the most popular coil used, but many other shapes and architectures are available today. With coil-on-plug technology being used from the OEMs for nearly 20 years, the aftermarket is finally offering improved coils for many of the most popular engines, among them the GM LS engine, the Ford Mod Motors, the Coyote platform, and the new Hemi.

Resistance

Resistance works against the current and is measured in ohms. It can be used to increase or decrease the flow of the spark energy. Coils can be wound with different materials and in different manners to alter the resistance of the primary and secondary windings, thereby modifying the output of the coil. Thicker material generally produces less resistance, which also means less heat. Of course, thicker material means a larger and heavier coil. With coil design, there is always a trade-off.

Primary windings have a much lower resistance value than secondary windings. Generally, the primary resistance of any coil is less than 2 ohms. In fact, it's usually in the tenths or even hundredths of an ohm in the case of coils designed for high-end CD ignitions. With

Performance replacement coils that fit factory brackets and connectors are now available for many popular applications. These coils may share the same housing as the stock version, but they're designed with improved materials and may have different windings to produce more output.

In the disassembled canister coil on the left, the iron center core and the windings are clearly visible. The windings of the E-shaped iron core on the right produce compact coil resulting in inductance efficiency with less voltage loss and less heat.

lower resistance, more current is in the windings when the field is collapsed and induced into the secondary windings.

Because thousands more windings are on the secondary side of the coil, there's bound to be more resistance. Depending on the coil, there may be 100 ohms or as many as 10,000 ohms. That's quite a range, but again it depends on the coil's working environment and what it supports. In addition, the windings must fall within the given specs of the turns ratio. One adjustment in a coil's buildup will affect several other specifications.

Inductance

The transfer of voltage and energy from one set of windings to the other is called inductance. It is measured in Henrys (H) and in the case of most automotive coils, in millihenries (mH).

Inductance is related to the charge time (rise time) of a coil. That is, the amount of time it takes for the voltage to be induced and increased through the secondary windings. The lower the inductance value, the faster the rise time. In high-end applications, changing from a high-inductance coil (slow rise time) to a low-inductance coil, the actual timing can be affected at higher RPM. If a coil doesn't take as long to induce a voltage, especially at higher RPM, you may see an advance in the timing.

To see a timing change, there must be substantial difference in the coils, but with the number of different coils available, it can happen. You may not see this change occur while revving the car in the pits. A load has to be on the engine so the coil builds up a higher voltage. When the engine is just revving freely, it doesn't take a lot of voltage to jump the plug gap, so the timing may not be affected as much. These kinds of changes are generally found in extreme test measures such as on a spin fixture and pressure chamber.

Housing Design

In the past decade, more coil designs have come from OEMs and the aftermarket. In most performance applications the coils are square, or have departed from the standard cylindrical or canister housing. This is due to advances in manufacturing and winding technology, that is, in the way the primary and secondary windings are laid out in relation to the iron core.

In many of these coils the core resembles an "E" compared to a straight piece of metal, hence the name E-core coils. This design

Ballast Resistor

When a breaker points distributor is used to open the primary coil circuit, a ballast resistor or resistance wiring is in line to the coil positive wire. This is necessary to lower the amount of voltage and current and that improves the longevity of the points. Most electronic triggers do not require the extra resistance because they can accept the increased current and voltage.

If a ballast resistor is in line to the coil's primary terminal, a bypass wiring circuit may occur during cranking. A wire running from the starter solenoid to the coil's positive terminal indicates the circuit, which is responsible for applying full battery voltage to the coil when the engine is cranking. The intent is to create a hotter spark to improve starting. Once the engine fires and the key is moved back to the run position, the only voltage going to the coil is through the ballast, where it is again regulated to a lower voltage, generally around 9.5 to 10.5 volts.

When some aftermarket coils are used with a points distributor, an extra ballast resistor is necessary. This is due to the coil's lower primary resistance, improved materials, and increased turns ratio. If one of these coils is used without the ballast, the points wear and burn prematurely.

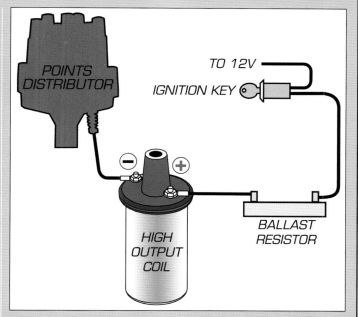

If you use a distributor with breaker points, an extra ballast resistor may be required to install a performance coil. The resistor lowers the voltage and current so the points aren't damaged.

has proven to be more efficient in increasing the voltage between the windings, due to a smaller and more enclosed area where the field collapses. Reducing the amount of leakage inductance (loss of energy) improves the coil's ability to transfer voltage and current to the secondary windings.

Another important aspect of a coil is how well it cools. Canister coils are generally filled with oil to keep the windings cool during operation. E-core coils are more efficient, so generally less heat dissipates, but they also produce more energy and voltage to begin with. Most E-coils use special heat-sinking materials to pull the heat out of the coil and into their grounded coil brackets and external housings. Another benefit to epoxy-filled E-coils is the added vibration protection achieved by encasing all of the wiring, so they cannot succumb to excessive vibrations. They also can be mounted in pretty much any position.

What's Available?

Aftermarket manufacturers offer a variety of coils. All of them have several improved-output replacement coils for the popular Ford TFI ignition module, dual connector GM coils, HEI coils, a few distributorless coil packs, and even coil-on-plug applications. The venerable canister coil is still offered in a variety of outputs and housings, but many other offerings are available these days.

When it comes to performance, each company has its own way of thinking, its own process for building a coil, and its own goals for what it wants the coil to accomplish. With an understanding of how a coil works and what it can do, you can find the right one to match your application, whether it's a cruiser, dedicated drag car, or road-course racer.

For instance, if you have a high-revving, small-block super comp engine with high compression that routinely sees 9,500 rpm, you need a coil with extreme voltage output and lightning-quick recovery time. However, that ignition and coil

MSD and Moroso recommend routing a ground wire from the coil's bracket to ground on their HVC and Plasma Plus coils, respectively. This extra ground (on the top right mount) is required to help suppress electromagnetic interference (EMI) and reduce the chance of shocks.

combination is not going to be ideal for a lower-compression, big-block that only reaches 6,500 rpm. This kind of application may benefit from less voltage, but longer spark duration.

Most ignition companies offer a variety of coils designed to work with their ignition systems. Crane recommends its PS92N coil for use in long-duration, high-RPM racing when coupled to the HI-6N ignition control.

HEI Hop Up

The GM HEI distributor uses a coil that is mounted inside its cap. This simple and efficient design for stock vehicles is a favorite of many street rodders. However, having the coil inside the cap can limit the voltage output potential due to size constraints and heat.

A variety of aftermarket coils bolt right into the cap. Some are designed to work with a stock or mild upgrade in the ignition module, such as the models available from Crane and Moroso. Others may be matched to a company's specific performance HEI module.

When you're swapping from a factory coil to an aftermarket version, make sure to use a coil that has the same-color wires that lead to the cap connector.

Another option is possible. Rather than just replacing the HEI with another HEI-style coil, remove it completely. Several companies offer a modified cover for the HEI that is made to transfer the high voltage from the coil to the rotor. This way you can run a coil with higher output that can be mounted outside.

MSD's HEI coil is designed to fit in place of the stock coil and even looks the same. Looks can be deceiving, though, and MSD recommends using their HEI coil only with their high-output HEI ignition module.

Some companies offer kits that allow you to remove the factory HEI coil and adapt an external coil to provide the high voltage. An extension leads from the center terminal rotor button out to a secondary tower.

In the Crane LX line the coils are smaller than in PS versions. This coil is designed exclusively for CD ignition systems such as Crane's HI-6 series and should not be used on inductive systems.

MSD has the capability to build several of their coils in-house, giving them the opportunity to evaluate different materials and winding procedures. Their Pro-Mag 44 and HVC II (high voltage and current) coils are built in-house. These coils have a serious amount of girth, but that is part of the reason that they produce such good output numbers. Like a racer with a good cam, MSD doesn't give out much info on the internals of any of their coils.

Troubleshooting Coils

There are not a lot of checks for the ignition coil, especially with an intermittent misfire. Typically, a coil is one of those things that either works or doesn't work, without a lot of middle ground.

You can check the primary and secondary resistance values of the coil, plus make sure they are not shorted to the housing or ground. Because there are so many different coil specifications, consult with your coil manufacturer to make sure everything is within spec.

To check the primary resistance, simply connect an ohmmeter across the coil's negative and positive terminals. The reading is generally less than 1 ohm. Connect your meter to the coil's secondary tower and one of the primary terminals to check the secondary resistance. Depending on the coil, this can measure from 30 to more than 1,000 ohms

Also check for continuity from the primary and secondary terminals to the coil's housing or ground to make sure there are no shorts.

Take a look around the secondary tower for signs of carbon tracking, which is caused by sparks arcing. While you have your ohmmeter out, check the resistance of the coil-wire lead to the distributor. Remember, this wire has to do four, six, or eight times the work that the other wires do. If it has excessive resistance or an opening, the voltage is going to find somewhere to get to ground, and that could mean jumping to the primary terminals or across to the engine.

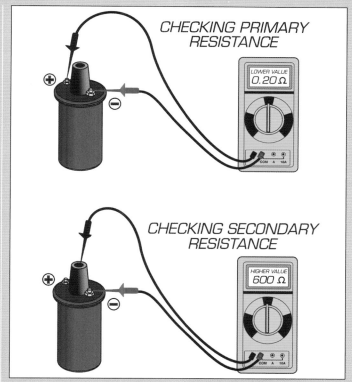

You can check the primary resistance value of your coil by connecting an ohmmeter across the primary terminal. To check the secondary resistance, connect it from the secondary tower to the primary positive terminal. Be sure you know your coil's specifications because they vary from manufacturer to manufacturer.

- Crane has specialty coils for street performance as well as a line of circle track–specific ignitions.
- Moroso offers an inductive and CD-designed coil in their Plasma Pulse Coils.
- Mallory offers several canister coils and has expanded the Promaster coil line with models for the Unilite distributors, for inductive systems, and even for high-RPM CD racing models. Malory also offers several E-core coils as Promaster E-Series for those same ignition designs.

The important thing to consider when selecting a coil is its compatibility with your ignition. It is recommended to stick with one company for an ignition and a coil, since they were intended to operate together. This is more common in street cars because once you get into competitive racing, teams try anything to get an inch ahead. If they find a different coil gives them two more horsepower with a different ignition control, you can bet they're going to run with it. There's even a chance of noticing timing differences when trying different models at this high-level (and high-RPM) range.

Always contact the manufacturer if you have coil compatibility concerns.

Spark Plug Wires

You can have the best coil and ignition controls available, but they won't do you any good if the spark plug wires aren't up to the task of handling their energy and voltage. Good plug wires are needed in all ignition systems, even distributorless types. As usual, exceptions exist; Ford and Chrysler engines no longer use plug wires. These systems have individual coils, hence the name coil-on-plug. These are mounted just above the spark plug, making the job of the plug wire obsolete. Again though, for this discussion, spark plug wires are an important part of assembling a performance ignition system.

When voltage travels through the spark plug wire, it creates a field. This magnetic field can wreak havoc on other electronics in your car, such as RPM limiters, timing controls, and even the ECU. To combat this EMI, or noise, a spark plug wire must use a conductor that has the ability to suppress this noise. This is why spark plug wires have resistance.

OEM's have been using spark plug wires with a carbon core for some years now. The carbon core serves as an adequate conductor, and it has very high noise-suppression capabilities. The trouble is that carbon core wires generally have extremely high resistance, even thousands of ohms per foot. High resistance means that the flow of the ignition's current is not optimum and could be reducing

MSD's HVC II coil line consists of two similar-looking coils. One is designed for use with an inductive ignition (left); the other is directed toward CD racing ignition systems (right). You can get away with an inductive coil with a CD ignition, but not with an inductive ignition. MSD offers numerous coil choices for all purposes.

The Mallory Promaster (PN 28880) coil is designed for their CD systems, including the HyFire VII and X electronic ignition controls. It is ideal for high-RPM applications that run for a long time.

Spark plug wires are the arteries of the ignition system and have a lot of things working against them, including underhood temperatures, wind, oil, gas, and exhaust heat.

MSD uses dual-crimp terminals to deliver a stout grasp on the wire: two sets of crimp tabs, one to grip the sleeve of the wire and the other to secure the conductor on each wire. These terminals also feature a locking tab that clicks onto the spark plug so you know when it is fully connected to the tip of the spark plug.

the amount of voltage that reaches the spark plugs.

Before there were so many electrically controlled components on racecars, having a solid-core wire was the ticket. Solid-core wires have no resistance, so you knew that the most energy possible was reaching the spark plug gap. Trouble started with the addition of higher-output ignitions, electric water and fuel pumps, electric fans, data acquisition, RPM limiters, timing controls, and other electronic devices. All of a sudden, the carrying capabilities of solid-core wires were fraught with noise interference.

Spiral-Wound Wires

The answer to your interference problem is to use spark plug wires that incorporate materials with resistance

Radio Noise

If you get an annoying buzz through the speakers with the radio on, it could be coming from the secondary side of the ignition, specifically, the plug wires.

Radio frequency interference (RFI) is noticeable mostly on the AM band and slightly on the FM band. This is one reason you need a good-quality spark plug wire. If you just installed a set of wires and notice a noise through your favorite tune, you should check out the installation. Another thing you can do is to apply a dab or two of dielectric grease on the plug boots and terminals. This helps reduce voltage leaks. Finally, make sure the ground is good from the engine to the chassis and from the stereo to the chassis.

If the noise is also audible when you're playing a tape or a CD, the culprit is more likely supply-line interference. For this type of interference, installing a noise filter or capacitor (available from manufacturers) on your new ignition's power leads will help. Not only can this help reduce noise, it also protects the ignition from voltage spikes and current surges.

Some dielectric grease (left) and a noise filter (right) for the ignition can help diminish radio frequency interference.

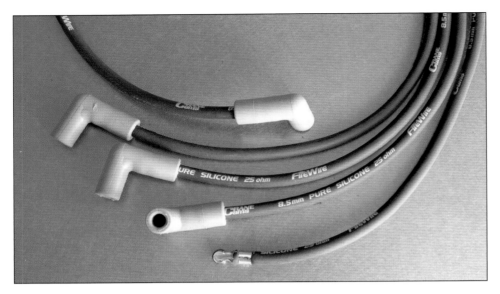

Crane's FireWire has only 25 ohms of resistance per foot, but still has high suppression capabilities. It features a silicone jacket to withstand high heat. It is also offered with a special heat sleeve for even more protection.

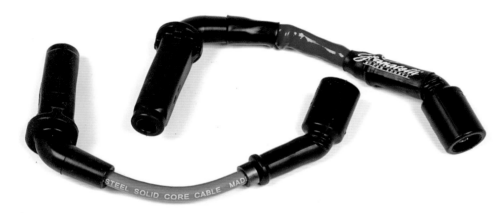

Solid-core wires typically are not recommended due to their inability to suppress EMI. Granatelli Motorsports, however, uses a solid stainless-steel conductor with a unique suppression technology in a 0-ohm wire for LS engines.

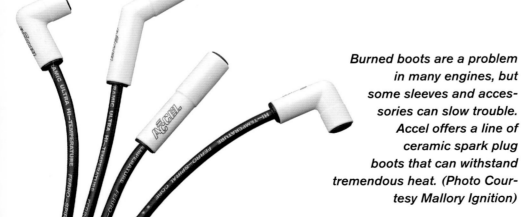

Burned boots are a problem in many engines, but some sleeves and accessories can slow trouble. Accel offers a line of ceramic spark plug boots that can withstand tremendous heat. (Photo Courtesy Mallory Ignition)

and that are designed to help suppress EMI. This sounds easy enough, but the trouble is that when a wire's resistance increases, it reduces the amount of voltage and current that reaches the spark plug. As resistance in the wire lessens, you increase the chances of EMI.

It's another one of those catch-22 ignition-system quandaries. The answer is a wire designed with lower resistance that can still suppress EMI; a wire that lets you have the best of both worlds. Is that too much to ask? Not any more! Companies have found ways to deliver a wire with lower resistance and higher suppression capabilities. These wires are referred to as helical- or spiral-wound plug wires.

The conductor material, usually stainless steel, nickel, or copper alloy, is actually wrapped around a center core. This center section of the core is made up of different materials designed to improve suppression capabilities. Most premium performance wires promote a core that is impregnated with ferrite or feature a semi-reactive core element. This means that the core has some degree of magnetic permeability or ability to establish magnetic induction. Winding the conductor around these special cores creates an effective higher EMI choke or suppression capability in addition to producing lower resistance wires that deliver higher spark energy. These new wires are a win-win.

As with most rules, some people just have to break them. Granatelli

Motorsports offers GM LS wire sets using a solid-core wire. Using patented technology, it's able to use a solid stainless-steel core short wire with 0 ohms of resistance. These wires are also able to operate with no interference to the vehicle's ECU or noise on the radio circuit.

Most wires from the aftermarket do a pretty good job. You're likely not going to feel a difference in performance going from a 100-ohm/foot wire to a 25-ohm/foot wire. Most wires range from less than 1,000 ohms/foot to Crane's

Building a Wire

You can buy a set of custom-made wires for your application, but when you want a set that is routed exactly how you want it to be, go with a universal set, and build them yourself.

Most universal sets are supplied with the spark plug side terminal and boot installed. This is good as you get the benefits of a strong factory crimp on the end you often pull off and on. The terminals and boots for the distributor side are supplied loose so you can cut each wire to your required length.

Cutting, stripping, and crimping the wires correctly is critical to the performance and life of the new wires. Most universal sets are supplied with a crimping tool designed to live through one or maybe two sets of wires. These will do, but if you plan to make more wires, you need to invest in a good-quality crimping tool. Moroso and MSD offer great tools that also have replaceable jaws, so you

can use the tool for other wiring purposes. Here are a few wire-building tips:

- Use extreme care not to damage or cut into the conductor. Any break in the conductor could promote an area for voltage to leak.
- After cutting the sleeve, strip it, and rotate the cut portion clockwise as you pull it off. The sleeve is lightly joined to the conductor, and this helps remove it without damaging the conductor.
- Use a dab of dielectric grease, such as MSD's Spark Guard, to protect against moisture and voltage leaks. It also makes assembly of the boot on the wire much easier.
- Do not over-crimp the terminal. You do not want the crimp tabs to tear into the sleeve. This may also promote an area for voltage to escape.
- Check the wire's resistance after assembling it. Better to find a bad crimp now than once the wires are installed on the car.

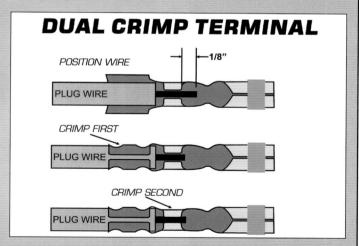

Most universal kits are supplied with a crimp tool that requires a vise or pliers. Investing in a quality crimp tool like this one makes your custom wires more professional looking and effective. It also saves you time and effort.

DUAL CRIMP TERMINAL

POSITION WIRE   ←1/8"

PLUG WIRE

CRIMP FIRST

PLUG WIRE

CRIMP SECOND

PLUG WIRE

These diagrams show how to position the conductor when using a dual-crimp terminal.

25-ohm/foot FireWire. The conductor is the most important part of a wire; the advertised thickness of the sleeve is not.

This is not to say that the sleeve isn't important. Obviously, a thick outer sleeve provides more protection to the conductor of the wire, but it does not affect the voltage-carrying properties. The outer sleeve of the wire takes the brunt of the engine heat, abrasion, and your oily, dirty hands. Most wire manufacturers use a form of silicone or their own proprietary compound to make up the outer sleeve of their wire.

Under this sleeve is another thick layer that adds greater electrical insulation to isolate the voltage. This is one area where the thicker wires can offer increased dielectric strength. A variety of materials are used here, but the latest and greatest seems to be ethylene propylene diene monomer, or EPDM. Look for a good-quality wire from the inside out.

Any old roll of wire sitting on your workbench won't do the job of transferring voltage. The wires need to have terminals and boots attached to each end, and this is another important area. You want to make sure that the terminals will securely grip and lock to the spark plug and cap terminal. Nothing is worse that having a wire come off during a race. Yanking on a wire while trying to remove it from the plug and having the terminal come off is almost as bad. Always twist the boot back and forth while pulling it off the spark plug.

Spark plug boots probably have one of the worst jobs of the ignition system. Boots need to handle extreme heat from headers and manifolds as well as keep the spark isolated so it goes into the spark plug rather than jumping to ground. All manufacturers deliver good-quality boots, but some applications can just be brutal. With boots, you get what you pay for. Be sure to review the boot material, construction, and feel before making a final decision.

Many companies offer a racing boot kit that is designed to handle more heat. Accel offers spark plug boots made from a special ceramic material.

Accessories

Take care of your wires by securing them from engine heat sources, add extra heat sleeving, and number them. These simple things will help

Taking extra precaution to protect and secure the wires ensures their long life and durability. Performance Distributors offers complete race-prepped wire sets that feature a durable heat sleeve and cylinder number indicators.

Billet aluminum wire looms are great for street rods, but you're probably not going to see them on too many racecars.

keep your wires, and your ignition's performance, in top condition. Most companies offer a variety of components to help you get the most out of your spark plug wires ranging from added boot protection to thick heat sleeves.

Moroso offers boot sleeves that are ideal for racing or even for use in a tow-rig application. These sleeves are made from 3M Nextel, a woven ceramic material that can withstand extreme conditions without damage or becoming brittle. Most ignition companies provide rolls of a durable silicone and glass woven sleeve that you slide over the wire for added heat and abrasion protection.

A set of separators is another important accessory for your spark plug wires. Routing and securing the wires from moving parts, hot engine components, linkage, and even other wires are important to the performance and life of your wires. When you're at racing speeds, such as with a circle track car, a lot of wind pushes and swirls under the hood. Having the wires secure is an important step in bulletproofing the car. Separators range from simple clips that hold the wires together to elaborate billet models that bolt to the engine.

Wire Maintenance

Plug wires have their work cut out for them. They must carry a high amount of voltage over a hot, volatile area. The wires tend to be forgotten and may go without inspection or replacement over time when no problems are evident. Depending on your application and ignition system, the plug wires should be considered a routine maintenance item. This is especially true of the coil wire; it works up to eight times more than the other wires.

The plug wires carry a considerable amount of voltage and energy on engines running an ignition such as an MSD-8 or a high-output magneto. Just like any other part on a racecar, the wires wear. Resistance might increase, cracks or breaks in the conductor could occur, and the

These separators do a good job of securing the wires. They can be screwed into place and they hold the wires even when their locking top is removed, which makes replacing or removing a wire easy.

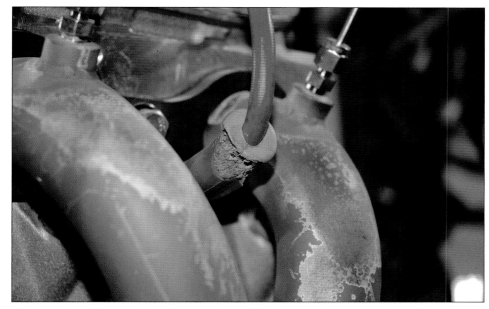

A close visual inspection of your wires will give you clues as to how they're holding up. Tears, cuts, or melted areas should be obvious, but also look for signs of burned spots where a spark could jump to ground. You can also check the resistance of the wires. Consult the manufacturer to find out the per-foot resistance value; all wires should read close to one another.

terminals wear from being pulled off and on during pit thrashes. How often you change your wires depends on how often the car is raced, but in extreme conditions, you want to inspect the wires every couple of events. Possibly replace the entire wire set once per year for bracket cars and sportsman racing.

Spark Plugs

The last part of the secondary side of the ignition, and the end of the ignition cycle, is the spark plug itself. In the past decade the number of spark plugs with different electrode materials and designs has grown rapidly. All manufacturers state that their spark plugs are the best design with ideal results in economy and performance. It can be difficult to wade through the marketing hype and get down to the real issue of performance. In the end, it seems that most ignition companies recommend a good-quality, standard-type spark plug for mild/performance applications.

For daily driving, the multiple-electrode versions and long-lasting platinum designs have benefits in late-model engines and last longer. However, for higher performance and racing, they're not ideal. Most OEM or replacement platinum plugs are designed for factory-type ignition systems and are not ideal for dissipating the added heat of a performance ignition. If you've moved to a nitrous system on a new Mustang, for example, you are limited in design but need a colder plug.

When it comes to racing engines, your builder can recommend a plug for a normally aspirated, blown, or nitrous-induced engine. Cost also becomes a factor when replacing

plugs several times throughout a race season, as some of these trick electrode plugs reach several dollars each.

The materials and combustion side of plugs have changed through

the years, but they still install and work pretty much the same. The spark plug wire connects to the center terminal of the plug. The energy is transferred from the wire through

The plug wires need to be considered a maintenance item on your racecar. At least replace the coil wire now and then. Which ignition system you use and how often you race dictate when the wires should be replaced.

Types of spark plugs include extended tips, multiple-electrode models, cold or hot models, resistor plugs, and more.

the center electrode of the plug (the core) to its tip in the combustion chamber. From there, it has to jump across a gap to the electrode, which is grounded to the metal shell of the plug, and to the cylinder head. Combustion of the air/fuel mixture occurs when the spark jumps the gap. Heat is also transferred from the spark plug to the cylinder head through the shell.

The shell of the housing is steel and provides a ground path between the electrode and the cylinder head. In most passenger car spark plugs, a resistor in the center electrode helps prevent EMI from interfering with the radio or other electronics. This is another reason you need a good set of spark plug wires that help suppress noise. Race engines generally use non-resistor plugs, as they're not concerned with a little radio static.

The center electrode and ground tip seem to be where manufacturers focus their designs. From left to right are: standard AC Delco plug, NGK with a small iridium-tipped electrode, Autolite with a cut-back ground electrode, and E3 edge-to-edge.

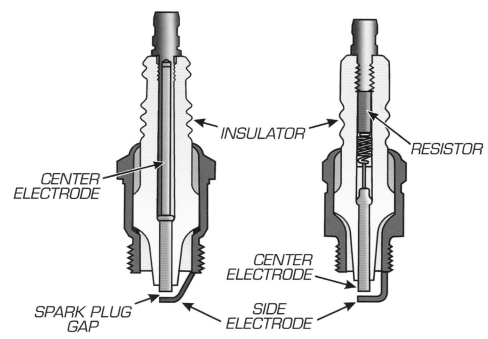

There's much more in the makeup of a spark plug than meets the eye. The center electrode must be well insulated and sealed to keep the spark from jumping to ground before it reaches the combustion chamber. Note the resistor in the center electrode, which helps reduce EMI.

Heat Range

You've probably heard about hot and cold plugs. They actually do not make a difference in an engine's performance output, but they can be of help when tuning. This means that using a hot or cold plug may result in better numbers, so they are indirectly related to output.

The heat range of a plug refers to its ability to dissipate the thermal load that occurs from compression. You need a plug with a heat range that rids itself of carbon deposits but doesn't create pre-ignition of the air/fuel mixture. If you use a plug that is too cold, you could be working toward early plug fouling due to excessive carbon buildup.

Manufacturers determine the heat range of their plugs through different materials as well as through the design of the insulator. A hot plug exposes more of the insulator material so it absorbs and retains heat rather than transfer it to the cylinder head. A cold plug has less insulator material exposed to the combustion event, so more heat is transferred to the head.

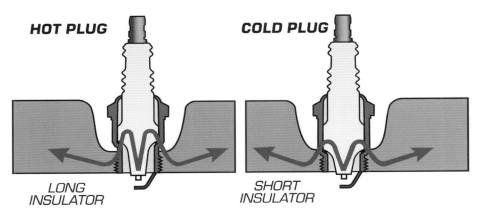

A cold spark plug has a shorter insulator tip to promote quicker dissipation of the heat through the shell and ground. The longer insulator on a hot plug retains the heat. This makes the hotter plug more capable of keeping clean in a rich-running engine.

Generally, the higher the number on the spark plug, the hotter the plug. An R45TS AC plug is two grades hotter than an R43TS. Always start with a cooler plug if you're unsure, because if you're wrong in your choice, the plug will show signs of being rich, which is a much better alternative than going too hot and experiencing detonation.

Typically, when you install a high-output ignition, you can choose a colder spark plug, but it is not necessary. If you're introducing nitrous to the combustion chamber you should definitely choose a cooler plug.

Another change you can make with plugs is the gap. Because your ignition now has the capability to produce higher voltage and current, opening the plug gap exposes more spark energy to the air/fuel mixture and that will result in improved combustion and more power.

Plug Gap

Plug gap is an important setting. You want the gap as large as possible to get the most spark energy exposed between the electrodes. However, there is a point of diminishing returns. When the gap is too large the spark has trouble jumping to the ground. In addition, a larger plug gap causes more pressure on the secondary side of the system and can even increase EMI or radio noise.

A weak spark or too much cylinder pressure can cause a failure to light the air/fuel mixture. A plug gap of .045 inch doesn't work well in a turbocharged engine that produces 25 psi of boost into the cylinder. Reducing this gap is necessary, but the determining factor is the ignition.

It is difficult for an ignition manufacturer to recommend a plug gap for every application. A typical street-driven, small-block Chevy can range from .030 to .050 inch. On blown-alcohol applications, plug gaps may be as small as .015 inch. On a street/strip car, after installing a CD ignition control, most manufacturers recommend opening the plug gap a little bit.

Start by opening it by .005 inch and test, and then try another .005 inch. When a change in performance no longer exists, go back .005 inch and call it good. If you see no improvement, stick with a gap just a little wider than the original. Remember, opening the gap also puts more pressure on the plug wires, cap, rotor, and coil wire.

Inspecting your plugs closely after a pass can give you an idea of what's going on in each cylinder. You can inspect each plug to help determine if it's running lean or rich, and for signs of detonation. Remember that driving the car back to the pits after a pass will spoil your attempts at reading the plugs.

Inspecting the insulator of the spark plug tells you more about what is occurring in the cylinder. A magnifying tool like this one from Powerhouse helps you gain even more insight into the spark plug and inside the cylinder. (Photo Courtesy Powerhouse Products)

Tuning with Spark Plugs

With the number of different spark plugs available and the variety of materials used in their production, it is difficult to explain exactly what to look for on plugs. The type of fuel, and even power additives such as nitrous, will affect the plug's appearance. Obvious signs of fouling from rich conditions are carbon buildup or wet plugs; lean conditions show extremely white with signs of detonation in excessive cases. Reading plugs is almost an art form, but it is also a valuable tool that you can learn with time and experience.

Inspecting your plugs closely after a pass can give you an idea of what's going on in each cylinder. You can inspect each plug to help determine if it's running lean or rich, or for signs of detonation. If you drive the car back to the pits after a pass, it will spoil any attempt to read the plugs. Try to check the plugs immediately after the pass.

Indexing Plugs

Indexing the spark plugs determines the position of the electrode so it is in the best position to ignite the incoming fuel charge. On high-performance engines, it can also be necessary to provide clearance between a custom piston and the electrode. Many racers swear by indexing, yet others do not give it a second thought. Try it on your engine; you may like it.

Indexing washers, such as these from Powerhouse, change the location of the electrode when you install the plug. A .010-inch washer rotates the plug clockwise 105 degrees, the .021-inch washer achieves 210 degrees of rotation, and the .032-inch washer delivers 315 degrees of rotation. (Photo Courtesy Powerhouse Products)

If piston clearance is not an issue, you want to position the electrode so it does not shield the spark from the incoming fuel mix. Plug-indexing washers, (such as those from Moroso) can accomplish this. These washers come in different thicknesses, so the location of the electrode is changed when the plug is torqued into the cylinder head.

On the outside of the spark plug, mark the location of the electrode and install the spark plug to see where it ends up. Then use the different washers to get your desired position. As far as the best position for the electrode, the jury is deadlocked. Common sense dictates that the open end of the electrode should face the intake valve to form a direct path from the air/fuel mixture to the spark. That may have been the rule in the past, but with the modern racing heads with small combustion chambers or angled-plug combinations, the need for indexing plugs has lessened from a performance perspective. The advent of numerous spark plug electrode designs with multiple tips or side electrodes has lessened the need to index spark plugs.

ELECTRONIC ACCESSORIES
RPM AND TIMING CONTROLS

This chapter reviews various opportunities and components to help control an engine's RPM and timing. Most of these accessories are designed to operate with existing ignition controls and distributors. They are designed as add-on components so you don't need to upgrade the entire ignition system. A variety of RPM controls as well as timing controls to be used with boost, nitrous, activation switches, and many more are available. Chapter 7 discusses programmable ignitions that have many of these features and others built in.

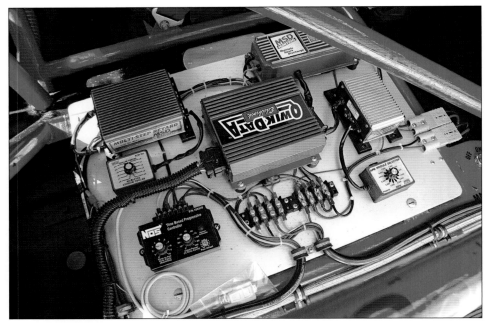

Once you have the ignition dialed in, plenty of timing controls and accessories can wire into the system. This racer has multiple retard steps, external rev limiters, a data recorder, and a time-based nitrous controller.

RPM Limiters

People don't usually think of an RPM limiter (also known as a rev limiter) as a means to improve performance, but using it off the line can help improve reaction times while providing consistent launches. You can also use RPM points for precise shift points, to activate a circuit, or even to turn on a nitrous solenoid. It all adds up to improved performance through consistency.

RPM limiters may not be a factor in finding more power from the engine, but knowing how your car and engine react to different RPM levels is important. Holeshot RPM and shift points help produce consistency, while an over-rev RPM limiter can save your engine.

RPM limiters were devised to help save engines from over-rev damage, but this technology was quickly employed for other tasks. Sure, most race cars on a road course or drag strip still have an RPM limiter for high-RPM protection, but when it comes to tuning, the RPM limiter is an important tool at the starting line.

A drag car is staged to leave the line and it sounds like rrrroooooo-daaaa-daaa-daaa-daaa-daaa *right before it launches with the wheels up. This is due to a two-step rev control. These components provide the ability to switch between a low RPM limit and the overrev limit.*

Drag racers were quick to realize the benefits of being able to activate different rev limits during the holeshot. This feature is most commonly referred to as a two-step RPM limiter. The two-step gives you the ability to switch between two different RPM levels. By activating an RPM limit on the starting line, you can improve consistency for bracket racing by tuning the suspension and car around a common holeshot RPM. An RPM limiter can also improve your reaction time, since you don't need to concentrate on the launch RPM. Simply push a button (on the clutch pedal or shift handle), put the pedal to wide open, and wait for the green light.

The two-step is a simple switching device. An activation wire for one of the limits is activated (generally by supplying 12 volts). This is usually accomplished by splicing the wire into the 12-volt feed line that connects to the trans brake or line-lock solenoid. When the Christmas tree goes green and the switch is released, the voltage is gone and the two-step switches to the high-side RPM limit for over-rev protection.

The common drag racer way of thinking is that if one is good, two are better, so three have to be even better, and so we have the three-step rev limiter. The idea in most cases is to be able to set a rev limit for use during the burnout. Some racers need more RPM during the burnout compared to the holeshot, so the third limit lets them achieve this. Not only does this keep the RPM lower than the high-side limit, but it can also aid in keeping tire temperatures within a consistent range.

Most new drag racing ignitions have a two-step built in, or there are accessories that give you the ability to add a two-step to your current ignition. In most cases, in order to add a two-step to your current CD ignition, the single rev limiter circuit must already be built in. You cannot add an MSD 2 Step Module Selector

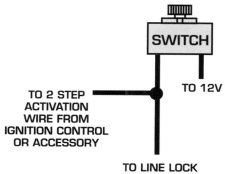

This diagram shows how easy it is to connect an MSD 2 Step Module Selector to your car. Depending on the transmission, you can either connect the low limit to be active with a transbrake or line lock switch.

Most two-step rev controls need access to an RPM socket on a CD ignition. The ignition has the rev-limiting circuitry and the step box simply acts as a switching device. With rotary dial rev-limit adjustments becoming more prevalent, this technology is changing but it is still commonplace.

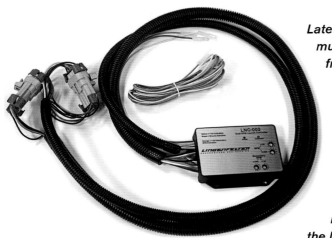

Late-model coil-on-plug muscle cars can benefit from a two-step launch control for consistent launches. This Lingenfelter Performance unit provides a launch RPM limit and over-rev setting for use on most GM LS engine platforms. Notice the rotary dials used to set the launch RPM limit.

to a 6A, because it does not have the rev-limiting circuitry in the ignition. Remember, the two-step is a simple switching device; all of the RPM-controlling circuitry is built into the ignition. Since a 6AL or 7AL-2 already has the MSD Soft Touch rev-controlling circuits, a two-step selector can be added.

Most two- and three-step devices simply plug into an ignition control

through the RPM module socket. There are, of course, exceptions to the rules. When MSD moved to the updated 6AL, it switched to a rotary dial-controlled rev limiter. This meant that the traditional two-step controller did not operate with the new box, so they had to develop a new model, the Digital 2-Step.

Late-model muscle cars such as the Camaro and Mustang have no simple aftermarket ignition controls. All new products had to be developed to give racers a way to set a starting-line rev limit. These versions plug into the factory coil harness and are

able to drop the cylinders and hold the RPM steady at the launch.

RPM Switches

If you want to activate a component at a certain engine RPM, you need an RPM-activated switch. These devices are extremely helpful when turning on a nitrous solenoid, activating an air shifter, or even for something as simple as turning on a shift light.

Several versions of these switches are available, but they all work in a similar fashion. They all connect to the tach signal of the ignition control and provide a ground path to complete a circuit at the specific RPM that you set.

Some models give you the option of supplying a ground path, or opening the ground path. One thing to watch for is activating a high-current component such as a nitrous solenoid, which requires you to wire in a relay. Many RPM switches can't handle much more than 1 amp of draw. Most switches can be used on four-, six-, or eight-cylinder engines, either with inductive ignitions or CD controls.

In the Clutch with a Holeshot Limit

So, you still like to stir the gearbox in your drag car (good for you!), but want to activate the two-step off the clutch switch. This can easily be accomplished with a micro-switch mounted off the clutch pedal. But wait a second. Won't the two-step be activated every time you push in the clutch? Yes, indeed it will, unless you get a little creative in your wiring with a relay. By wiring in a relay, you can activate the two-step rev limiter through the clutch switch and latch onto the line lock at the same time. This means that the clutch switch controls the launch RPM and the line lock at the same time. ∎

RPM Activated Switches can be handy devices to use to consistently activate a circuit at a specific RPM. They can be used to turn on a shift light, nitrous circuit, shifter, and any number of RPM-related items.

For distributorless ignitions with waste-spark systems, or coil-per-cylinder, the RPM signals are different. If you connect an RPM switch to a single coil while it's programmed for a V-8, the RPM value will be considerably off.

Check the manufacturer specs to make sure the switch fits your application.

Shift Lights

A shift light is basically an RPM switch coupled with a light or LEDs.

A shift light is basically an RPM-activated switch connected to a light of some sort. This model from MSD allows you to set the activation RPM on the side of the unit. When the engine reaches the desired RPM, the LED turns on to alert the driver to shift.

The idea behind a shift light is to alert a driver to shift and to do so with some consistency. The RPM level can be selected through plug-in modules or by programming. MSD, Auto Meter, and other companies offer several versions.

Shift lights are simple to install and they function with most inductive and CD systems, and on many cylinder options. They really just need a clean RPM signal, a ground, and 12 volts. Some of the newer LED or penlights are small enough to install behind a dashboard to hide and keep a factory look. Auto Meter offers several that work in concert with their tachometer offerings.

As more manufacturers and racers embrace computer technology, even more RPM controllers will become available for late-model vehicles.

Timing Control

Ignition timing is one of the most important tuning aspects in relation to your engine's performance and endurance. It can be controlled and adjusted through the distributor's centrifugal advance or even by physically moving the position of the distributor. But what about when you want to move it just a couple degrees for performance or need to retard the timing during a short blast of nitrous? Are you going to get out and swap a stop bushing or move the distributor? Probably not.

Being able to retard the timing is important in many cases, such as trying to avoid detonation, when using nitrous, high boost pressures, or even simply running at high RPM. Such systems can be beneficial in a

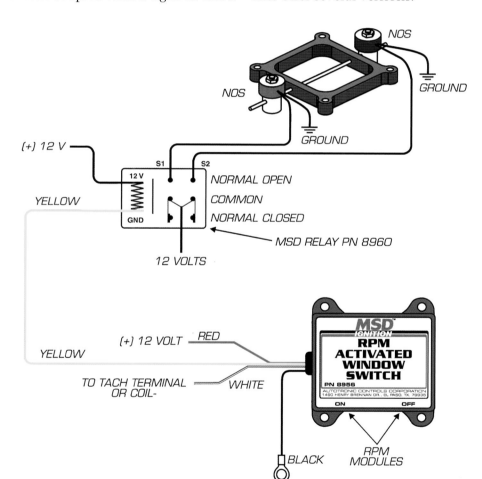

This diagram shows an MSD RPM Activated Window Switch wired to turn on a nitrous solenoid at 3,600 rpm. The "window" portion means it deactivates the same circuit at a higher RPM. In this case, it is set for 6,800 rpm, so it turns off the juice before the rev limiter kicks in (set at 7,000 rpm).

number of applications, even when you still use centrifugal advance of the distributor. The variety of electronic timing controls ranges from a simple rheostat that retards the timing with the engine running, to full-blown PC-based controllers with settings to adjust cylinder-to-cylinder timing, multiple timing curves, retard stages, and more.

A couple of different control types come in handy for street cars: electronic and rheostat.

Electronic

Electronic timing controls simply receive or intercept the trigger signal before the coil or ignition control to "pause" the signal through its circuitry, resulting in retarding the timing. One thing to understand here is that there is no way for a timing control to advance the timing. A control cannot sense a trigger signal before the magnetic pickup or Hall-effect switch sends it. You still need to set the total timing with your distributor or a crank trigger and retard the timing from that point.

MSD offers a timing control with a dash-mounted control knob so you can alter the timing as you drive down the road. Various models connect to factory inductive ignition systems or an aftermarket CD ignition control such as a 6A. Originally, this timing control was designed for tow vehicles. If they encountered times of detonation from changes in altitude or poor-quality gas, the timing could easily be retarded to dial away the detonation without stopping. It is a much better alternative to stopping the truck and burning knuckles to move the distributor! This setup can also be advantageous in performance applications.

If your street engine is on the verge of requiring high-octane gas, an adjustable timing control could be helpful. For daily or mild cruises you could simply retard the timing a few degrees by turning the control dial from the comfy confines of the driver's seat. When you're ready to get serious and hit the strip with some quality fuel, all you need to do is crank those few degrees right back in.

One of the most basic timing controls is from MSD. It ties in between the distributor and an external ignition control. From there, a dash-mounted control knob allows the driver to pull out timing without touching a wrench.

Rheostat

When using a timing control with a rheostat to change the timing manually, remember that the timing is retarded across the entire ignition curve. This includes the idle timing and the total timing after the centrifugal advance is all in.

When you're just cruising at moderate throttle and the vacuum advance is active, the retard is also active. An exception is if you are referencing boost pressure to determine the amount of timing retard. This example is especially important with forced-induction systems.

Boost Retard

There is just no way around it: Blowers and turbos are cool. They make awesome power and look great on any engine, but when you're running one you need to pay attention to what your timing is doing. When the air and air/fuel mixture is being forced into the cylinder from a turbocharger or supercharger, the performance output of the engine jumps right up. That performance stems from increased cylinder pressures, which also change the timing requirements of the engine.

As boost pressure increases, so does the need for a timing retard. MSD offers an ignition accessory, the Boost Timing Master (BTM), with which you can retard the timing via a dash-mounted control knob. This allows you to set how much timing the ignition should retard relative to boost pressure. You can set the dial to retard from 1 to 3 degrees for every pound of boost pressure. This feature is also built into their 6 BTM Ignition control so you get the benefits of high-voltage sparks, a rev limiter, and a boost timing control all in one unit.

Timing Controls: More Than Just a Timing Retard

A common question about timing controls is whether they're capable of advancing the timing. These controls cannot see into the future and know when to trigger the ignition before the actual switching device does. They are not designed to advance the timing, but there is a way to trick the system into thinking it can so you achieve a sort of electronic advance.

When a timing control offers 15 degrees of retard, you can actually get 7 of advance and 8 of retard. Simply move the distributor to advance the timing 7 degrees and lock it in place. Then, fire up the engine and set the timing back to its original setting through the control knob. If your adjustment is correct, the dial should indicate 7 degrees, and hocus-pocus, you have now advanced the timing as well as retarded it without even opening the hood.

This can be helpful in a car that sees double duty as a daily driver and weekend warrior. For bracket cars, it saves you the hassle of having to move the distributor around.

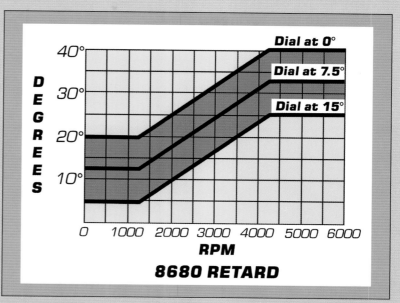

This chart shows how to cheat the timing control into thinking it can advance and retard the timing. By dividing the total amount of retard possible in half and moving the position of the distributor, you can effectively have a timing advance and a timing retard at your fingertips.

Blowers are cool to show off and a blast to drive, but you need to control the timing as boost pressures increase. A boost-retard timing control lets you select the amount of timing retard in relation to the boost pressure in the engine.

An electronic timing control can be used in place of the centrifugal advance mechanism in the distributor. This upgrade takes the place of weights, springs, and the stop bushing. Both electronic and centrifugal devices serve the same purpose (to match the timing with the engine's load and RPM), but electronic systems can deliver much more control, especially for high-performance applications. Some of the benefits are: They are more accurate, they can react faster, they are repeatable, and they allow you to set a variety of functions.

Locked-Out Timing

A time may come when your car is strictly for the racetrack, or at least more strip than street. When this transformation is realized, certain things no longer need to be considered. Power steering or air conditioning? No thanks. Quiet exhaust and decent economy? Nope. Centrifugal advance? No thank you; just lock it out.

Why would you want to lock out the centrifugal advance? Remem-ber that as RPM changes, so do the engine's timing requirements. Daily drivers need to idle smoothly, start in hot conditions, and maintain good drivability with varying loads. Your racecar is designed to excel under one condition only: wide open. In this case, why even deal with the centrifugal advance when you are only concerned with total timing?

If you're going to make the move to complete electronic control over the timing, the first thing you need to do is lock out the distributor.

Locked-out timing refers to having only total timing (no vacuum or centrifugal advance added), which is accomplished by locking out the advance mechanism. This means strip the weights, springs, and components off the distributor and weld it together. For most aftermarket distributors, no welding is required: they're designed to lockout with minimum work.

This is also a good time to consider a crank trigger to fire the ignition. I discuss this later in this chapter.

Let's say you have the timing locked at 36 degrees. This means that a lot more pressure is on the starter, flexplate, and battery when you try to start the engine, especially after a hot soak on a thick summer day. Advanced timing is not starter friendly and is even worse with a hot engine. This is because the spark is starting the combustion process earlier in the piston's combustion stroke, and the engine is only at 200 to 250 rpm during cranking.

The only inertia the piston has going for it is from the starter, and the advanced combustion process puts a lot of pressure on the slow-moving piston. This is one of the main reasons that a centrifugal or electronic advance is built into most distributors.

The Boost Master makes changing the timing as easy as turning the radio up. It is an add-on control that allows you to pull out timing relative to boost pressures. This type of control is ideal for higher-performance street engines that require a little less timing to avoid detonation.

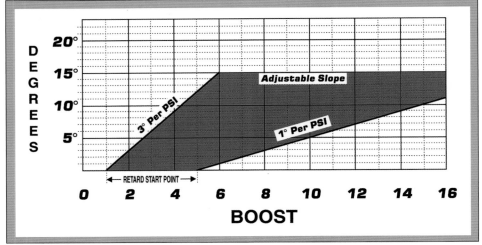

This chart shows the relationship between the engine's boost pressure and the amount of timing retard that you can adjust.

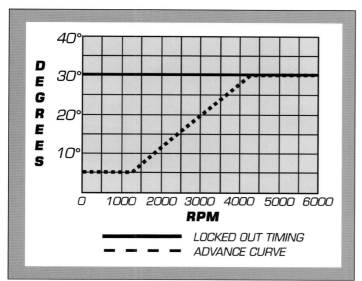

LOCKED OUT TIMING
ADVANCE CURVE

The dotted line represents a typical centrifugal advance curve compared to the solid line showing locked-out timing. The locked-out timing may fit racecars but is not a street-friendly route due to increased cranking pressures, varying engine loads, and idle speeds.

For racecars, this problem can be overcome with a stout gear-reduction starter and strong battery that remains charged between rounds. In addition, other electronic accessories are available that provide a retard while the engine is cranking.

The Starter Saver is a compact device that plugs into the magnetic pickup from the distributor and sends the trigger signal back to the ignition control. It provides either 10 or 20 degrees of retard when the engine is cranking. As soon as the device senses 700 to 800 rpm, the timing goes back to the non-retarded, mechanically

Bolt Down to Lock Out

If you have an MSD Pro-Billet distributor with a mechanical advance, you can easily lock it out. First, remove the springs, weights, and their spacers. Then remove the lock nut that holds the stop bushing in place. Keep the nut handy; you'll need it again.

Next, remove the gear or retaining sleeve from the distributor shaft. (Ford distributors have gears that are pressed on, so just remove the sleeve.)

You only need to pull up the distributor shaft a couple of inches. Note the position of the little threaded stud where the stop bushing was originally located. Turn the shaft 180 degrees and put the threaded stud in the hole. Install the lock nut and you're officially locked out.

Notice anything missing? This distributor has been converted to lockout by the elimination of the springs, weights, and movement. Sometimes people even weld the advance plate to the shaft.

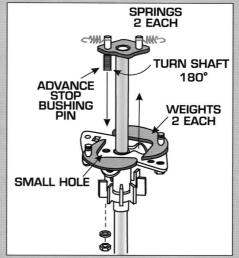

SPRINGS
2 EACH

TURN SHAFT
180°

ADVANCE
STOP
BUSHING
PIN

WEIGHTS
2 EACH

SMALL HOLE

Many aftermarket distributors allow you to easily lock out the timing. Once the springs and bushings are removed, you have to pull the gear or retaining sleeve off to rotate the shaft 180 degrees and bolt down the advance assembly. The nice thing about being able to lock out the distributor without welding it together is that the process is reversible if you ever decide locked-out timing isn't right for your engine.

When you switch to locked-out timing, the engine may experience hard cranking due to the spark occurring sooner on the compression stroke. A start retard device provides a few degrees of retard to ease pressure on the starter and flexplate.

For engines with multi-stage nitrous systems, a retard control with different stages is required to match the different amounts of nitrous being used. Retard rates are controlled with dials for each stage.

set amount. Thus, the pressure is eased on the starting components.

Another handy component from MSD is the Start/Step control. This unit lets you select the amount of retard that occurs during cranking in 5-degree increments from 5 to 20. It also has an adjustment for retarding the timing, that is, a step retard. A step retard is used primarily with nitrous to retard the timing only when the nitrous is activated. In this example, a rotary dial allows you to tune in a timing retard from 1 to 15 degrees.

Step Retard

A step retard control activates a step, or stage, of retard at a selected moment. An activation wire enables the retard step when you need it, for example, when a nitrous solenoid is turned on. This is the most common application because the introduction of nitrous and oxygen into the combustion chamber causes the engine to require less timing advance. Being able to enable a timing retard only when the nitrous system is active

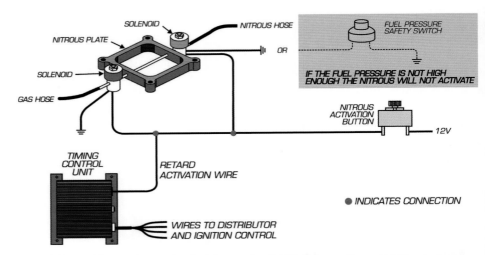

This diagram illustrates a single-step retard wired to a nitrous plate system. The retard is activated through the nitrous activation wire. A safety switch to monitor fuel or oil pressure is a smart, engine-saving addition. If either is too low, the nitrous doesn't turn on.

provides the best use of your ignition timing.

To control the activation of the retard step, the control has a corresponding wire that needs to be connected to 12 volts (in most cases) or removed from ground to retard the timing. (Be sure to check with the control's manufacturer on how to wire their system.) An example is to splice the activation wire into the

nitrous solenoid's switching 12-volt supply wire. This way, the timing is retarded as soon as the nitrous is activated.

Multi-step retard controls go along with multi-stage nitrous systems. Just as the name implies, multi-step retard controls provide several stages of retard. Generally, three or four separate retard steps, each with its own activation wire, connect to the corresponding stage. Depending on the system you use, these steps can be cumulative (activated together) or sequential (each stage cancels the other when activated).

For example, with a cumulative multi-stage nitrous system you may take out 8 degrees of timing with the first stage, 6 more with the second, and an additional 2 with the third stage for a total retard to 16 degrees at top end. Being able to program a different amount for each stage provides a lot of control over each stage.

If the tune-up changes and more nitrous is used during the third stage instead of the second, the amounts of retard can easily be switched.

If three is good, four must be better, right? The MSD Digital Multi-Retard offers four different retards that are adjusted with rotary dials rather than plug-in modules. It also offers an adjustable-start retard circuit.

Nitrous HP = Degrees of Retard

Nitrous oxide is made up of two nitrogen molecules and one oxygen molecule. That molecule of oxygen does wonders for performance when it is mixed properly with the correct amount of fuel. Remember, it's not the nitrous that makes the power; it's the extra fuel you can burn thanks to the oxygen.

In addition, the intake charge is cooled because the nitrous absorbs heat as it changes from a liquid state to a gas. This increases the density and oxygen content. The burn rate of the air/fuel mixture is increased, which means the timing must be retarded to compensate.

How much retard you need is dependent on how much nitrous oxide is being introduced. A rule of thumb is 2 degrees of retard for every 50-horsepower shot of nitrous. It is better to retard the timing too much than to not retard enough.

After an initial pass, pull all of the plugs (yes, *all* of them) to get an idea if you're too rich or a little lean. Cylinders can have slight variances in the way they perform, so it is important to check each spark plug.

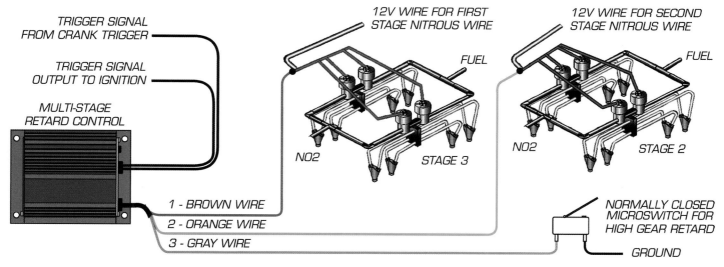

This is an example of a typical multi-step retard control wiring with a two-stage nitrous system. The control receives the trigger signal from the distributor, then sends it to the ignition control. The corresponding retard wires are sliced into each nitrous solenoid's 12-volt wires. When the nitrous solenoids are activated, the ground is removed and the retard step is activated. As soon as the nitrous is turned off, timing goes back to the normal setting.

When you retard 10 to 15 degrees or more of timing, you need to start thinking about phasing the rotor. This requires a crank trigger, but if you don't consider the rotor phasing there is a good chance of spark scatter or a misfire.

to pull out a couple degrees of timing at top end (or high RPM), which can be accomplished with a micro-switch on the shifter. Dirt track racers can be sneaky and have a switch to flip and pull a couple degrees out to soften the engine power as track conditions deteriorate. Others are doing just the opposite by putting timing back into the engine at high RPM in an effort to boost the engine's torque curve. This could be handled with an RPM-activated switch set up to turn off a retard at a desired RPM. Use your imagination!

A sequential retard control keeps each retard rate independent as they override one another. When the second stage is activated, the amount of retard pulled out by the first stage is deactivated, and the second stage retard rate is enabled. A third stage overrides both stage one and stage two.

This system can be beneficial if you decide to put timing back in at certain points. For instance, if you really want to kill some power coming off the line, you may retard the timing 15 degrees, then for the second stage it could be programmed for only 8 degrees because the car is rolling and the tires are already hooking up.

Most timing retards limit the amount of available retard to 25 to 30 degrees. The most important reason for this limit is rotor phasing. Rotor phasing refers to the relationship between the cap terminal and the position of the rotor tip when the ignition fires. The maximum amount of retard that a standard-size distributor cap and rotor can handle is approximately 25 degrees. You can make adjustments to ensure safe operation of a major amount of

retard, but it involves stepping up to a crank trigger system.

Of course, nitrous isn't the only application for which a step retard is used. Many engine builders like

Crank Trigger

If you've decided that locked-out timing is right for your application, then you should consider moving to a

When it comes to precise trigger signals, you can't beat a crank trigger system. Most distributorless ignitions receive their trigger signal from the crankshaft.

crank trigger ignition system. It is the most accurate way to trigger the ignition throughout high-RPM operation. Moreover, if you're frequently manipulating the ignition timing, you need to consider rotor phasing, which is much easier to set when triggering the ignition from a crank trigger.

A crank trigger system provides the same function as the pickup inside a distributor: to trigger the ignition control. The benefit of a crank trigger is that the trigger signal comes directly from the crankshaft, and no other engine component is more closely related to piston position and engine RPM. This system bypasses mechanical variables from vibration frequencies and flexing that occur through the timing chain, its gears (cam gear to distributor gear), and the distributor shaft.

Crank trigger kits are available from performance ignition companies. Most operate by installing an aluminum trigger wheel to the crankshaft dampener. On V-8 engines this wheel has four magnets positioned at 90-degree increments; six-cylinder engines have three magnets positioned at 120-degree increments. These magnets produce a signal that triggers the ignition as they spin past a stationary non-magnetic pickup mounted close to the edge of the wheel. Some companies use Hall-effect pickups.

Setting Up a Crank Trigger

Installing a crank trigger system is pretty straightforward, as most kits come with the brackets and accessories needed for a complete installation. One aspect to consider is that the trigger wheel bolts to the balancer, which means that the belt pulley is spaced farther out. You have to compensate for the extra width by

The non-magnetic pickup of a "flying magnet" crank trigger can only be triggered by the magnets in the wheel. This makes false triggering impossible due to track debris or other metal objects. Note the arrow on the wheel denoting rotation of the engine. The wheel must be installed correctly or the timing will be affected because of the position of the magnets and their polarity.

A non-magnetic pickup is similar to a coil. It has a coil of windings around an iron core that together produce a voltage signal when a magnet passes through its path.

The pickup must be aligned with the centerline of the trigger wheel's edge (as shown). Being off could adversely affect the strength of the signal. The air gap between the pickup and the wheel should be .035 to .060 inch and does not change the performance level of the engine.

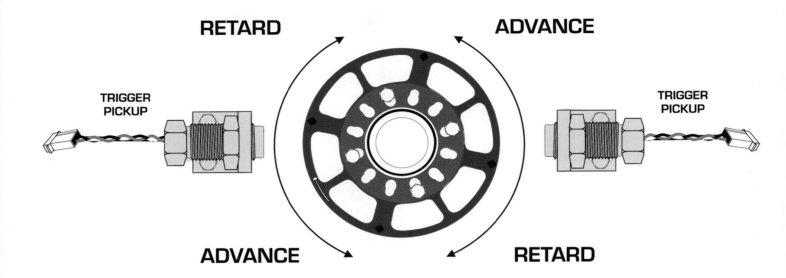

The ignition timing is adjusted by the position of the pickup. The direction you move it to advance or retard depends on the location of the pickup on your engine.

Because the timing is controlled by the crank trigger pickup, you only need to position the distributor so the number-1 cap terminal is aligned with the rotor tip when the engine is sitting at the desired timing.

moving any belt-driven accessories the corresponding distance.

One of the most important things is ensuring that the trigger wheel is centered on the balancer. Most trigger wheels have a couple of different bolt patterns as well as a centering ring for various applications. With the trigger wheel installed, mount the brackets and pickup. Usually spacers are supplied with the kit, so you can position the pickup on the centerline of the trigger wheel.

The next step is to adjust the gap between the pickup and the wheel. The air gap is not like a spark plug gap; it doesn't affect performance. The pickup needs to be close enough to create a trigger at cranking speeds. If the engine starts, the pickup is close enough. Conversely, big-cubic-inch engines at high RPM can have excessive crankshaft flexing, so you don't want the pickup to be too close to the contact point. The recommended gap is .035 to .060 inch.

To set the timing, position the number-1 cylinder at the desired timing BTDC. Slide the pickup until it is aligned with the closest magnet and tighten it in place. Also confirm that the number-1 spark plug terminal (at the cap) is aligned with the rotor tip. Start the engine and check the timing with a light. If the timing is off or is varying, check the wiring of the pickup, as the polarity of the wires must be correct. In many cases, if the polarity is swapped, the engine still starts but the timing fluctuates and dances all over.

Crank Trigger Distributors

Once you have a crank trigger handling the trigger chores, the distributor's responsibility is reduced to just distributing the spark. Of course, it is still important to have a solid housing and shaft assembly, but another benefit is that you can run a shorter distributor. This is a terrific option when firewall or exotic intake combinations make space a premium. Versions of these distributors can be smaller or shorter because they don't have to make room for a pickup or advance assembly. The rotor is simply connected to the distributor shaft along with a cap.

Some distributors have a Ford-style cap, which is desirable because of its large diameter. If things are too tight for this cap, Mallory and MSD offer distributors with a "crab cap." This cap features terminals that stick out of the side rather than out the top. This really opens up the area around the distributor. The downside is that the cap is quite small, but in many cases, it is the only answer. It works, but, again, going with a larger cap is always recommended.

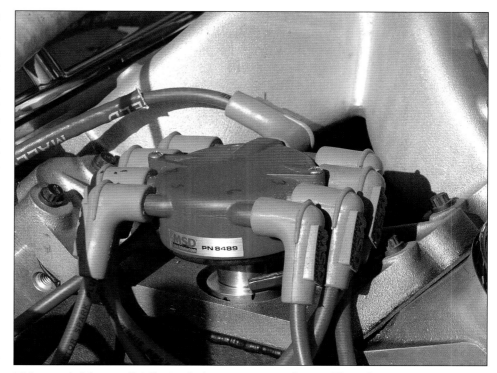

This crank trigger distributor is known as a crab cap. The wires come out on the side of the cap, providing more clearance around cowlings or firewalls. It's an added benefit of moving to a crank trigger system.

With no pickup or advance, crank trigger distributors can sit very low and be unobtrusive so there's more room for outlandish intake combinations.

Rotor Phasing

With a crank trigger, the distributor only has the simple task of transferring the high voltage from the coil to the correct distributor terminal at the right time. All you need to do is line up the rotor tip and the distributor cap terminal at your desired timing. This alignment is called rotor phasing. It sounds simple enough, but what happens when you manipulate the timing?

On engines that use electronic retard controls (such as those used with nitrous), rotor phasing becomes extremely important. When the timing is retarded, the spark occurs after the rotor tip passes the cap terminal. This means it takes more voltage to jump across the gap, which puts more pressure on the secondary side of the ignition. The spark may start looking for an easier path to ground, and that could result in a miss or crossfire to another cylinder.

On a single-stage nitrous system that only requires a few degrees of retard when the system is active, the rotor phasing will be slightly off, but as long as everything on the secondary side of the ignition is in good condition, it should not pose a problem. Remember that the number of degrees of change in the distributor is half that of the crankshaft. Depending on

Front Drive

If space is at a premium, you can go with a front-mount distributor. It mounts vertically to the front of the motor and is driven from a pulley and belt installed to the timing gear. Obviously, a belt-driven cam is required, so this system is primarily for high-performance racing engines.

Jesel and Comp Cams offer belt-drive camshaft kits, and Jesel offers a front-drive distributor to complete its kit. Moving to a front-mount distributor makes routing the plug wires easy. There's less heat to deal with, and the belt drive absorbs mechanical harmonics from the cam and crank.

The major gains in moving to a front-drive distributor are the added space at the rear of the engine (on traditional rear-mounted distributor engines). Other benefits are added clearance for exotic intake manifold combinations, fewer mechanical variables through the timing chain, and less valvetrain noise. In addition, swapping intakes becomes easier without having to bother with a distributor and rotor phasing, and inspection of the cap and rotor is also easier.

A front-drive distributor is a popular solution for tight engine compartments and intake setups. By using a belt drive on the camshaft, a front-drive distributor can be incorporated by running a belt off the camshaft to turn the distributor. Jesel, Mallory, and MSD all have front-mount distributor kits.

the size and condition of the cap and rotor, a retard of more than 8 degrees warrants concern with adjustment of the rotor phasing.

As the nitrous dose or even boost pressure gets larger, more timing needs to be pulled out. For instance, if a racer is pulling out 14 degrees of timing when the nitrous is activated, the rotor tip is well past the cap terminal when the ignition fires. So you already are putting higher pressures against the ignition system with the phasing off, not to mention the increased cylinder pressures from the nitrous being injected into the mix.

This all adds up to higher voltage necessary to jump the gap along with more reasons for a misfire. If you're at this level of performance, the rotor phasing must be checked and set.

On racecars, it is important that the rotor phasing be aligned when the engine is racing and all of the retard rates are active. It is easier for the phasing to be off a couple degrees when the engine is idling and cylinder pressures are low than when the engine is under increased cylinder pressures or at high RPM.

How much timing you are pulling out affects where to set the rotor phasing. A high-horsepower nitrous engine may require as much as 20 degrees of retard. In extreme cases such as this, it may be best to split the difference in the phasing. For example, if you are pulling out 15 degrees of timing, set the phasing at about 10 degrees (crankshaft degrees). This throws the phasing off 10 degrees at idle and low speeds, and at high RPM, it is only off by 5 degrees, which should not present problems.

Checking and Setting Rotor Phasing

To check the rotor phasing, locate an old distributor cap that you can modify. Choose a terminal that is easy to view while the cap is installed and the engine is running. Drill a hole large enough to see the plug wire terminal post and the rotor tip.

With the cap installed, connect a timing light to the spark plug wire that runs to the terminal you can see. With the engine running, you can see the position of the rotor tip as the spark jumps across to the wire, and you can align it correctly. Remember to activate any retard controls so you can see where the phasing is during a run down the track.

Can You Phase It?

Can rotor phasing be adjusted if you're using the pickup inside a locked-out distributor? The pickup inside the distributor is usually mounted in one place and is not adjustable. One of the few choices is to reposition the pickup, which takes time and a lot of machine work. An alternative is the adjustable rotor Cap-A-Dapt kit from MSD.

This kit fits many MSD distributors and most models that accept a GM points-style cap. The rotor has two pieces: a base and a top with slotted holes. This allows the phasing to be adjusted by rotating the top piece. You also get the benefit of a larger cap diameter for improved spark isolation.

MSD's Cap-A-Dapt with a two-piece rotor provides an easy way to set rotor phasing. Note the adjustment slots around the two rotor-retaining screws. In addition, the large-diameter cap lessens the chance of spark scatter within the cap.

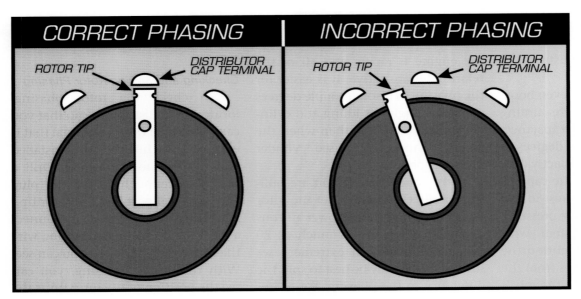

CORRECT PHASING	INCORRECT PHASING
ROTOR TIP · DISTRIBUTOR CAP TERMINAL	ROTOR TIP · DISTRIBUTOR CAP TERMINAL

These diagrams illustrate correct rotor phasing, and what happens when it is off. On distributors with small caps, you can see how easily the spark could jump to the next terminal, resulting in crossfire and possible pre-ignition.

Rotor Tips and Conditions

Another important component of rotor phasing is the condition of the rotor itself. Worn and burned tips and terminals do not make it any easier to get the lazy voltage to go to the right place at the right time. Voltage likes to build up on a sharp edge to jump a gap, so having a rotor tip in prime condition is important. In most cases, simply treating the cap and rotor as a maintenance item throughout the race season will suffice.

MSD found that on their high-output ignitions and magnetos, a special rotor tip increased the longevity and performance of the secondary side of the ignition. The rotor tip has one rounded corner and one edge at a right angle. An arrow denotes the rotation of the distributor. By positioning the rotor tip so the sharp corner is the trailing edge of the rotor's rotation, there is less chance of spark scatter. This tip is only available on MSD's extra-large Pro-Cap.

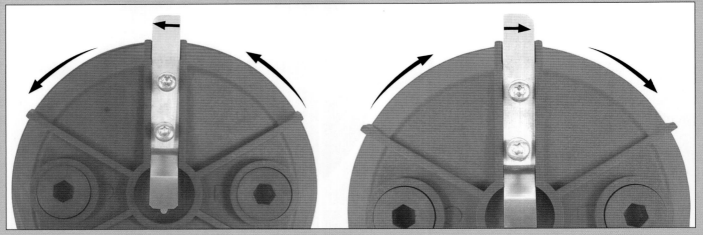

This special rotor tip was designed to improve the control of the voltage delivery on high-output race-only ignitions such as the MSD-8 or Pro-Mag 44. The tip is reversible, depending on your engine's rotation. It is also helpful when using timing retards.

ADVANCED IGNITION TUNING
PERFORMANCE FROM A PC

A variety of minute timing (or RPM) adjustments are possible for you to improve consistency, 60-feet track times, track control, and more. Chapter 6 discussed the use of add-on accessories and controllers. This chapter deals primarily with ignition systems that offer programmable features that are controlled through a PC or laptop.

Mechanical Cylinder Timing

No two combustion chambers are absolutely alike or require the same amount of timing. This is because of a variety of issues with intake manifold design and length, head material, valve location, spark plug type, and so on. The differences have always been more of a concern in advanced circle track racing. However, they're highlighted in extreme nitrous applications, because of the increased cylinder pressures and the introduction of more oxygen into the chamber.

What's the benefit of cylinder-to-cylinder timing? Consider the often-used adage, "One bad apple spoils the whole bunch." When you set the timing of your engine at 34 degrees, you are setting it at 34 degrees for every cylinder. That may not be ideal in every hole. If you have one or two cylinders that run leaner than the other cylinders, you have to compromise for these "bad apples." This results in the other cylinders running a touch off their ideal timing setting and your engine's output not being as much as it should be. Compromising power is not something that engine builders and racers ever want to hear about.

Circle track racers have been modifying the distributor's reluctor

Advanced tuning for the fuel management, ignition, and (in this case) the complete electrical system are achieved with a laptop rather than hand tools. Here, three different software programs are required, but in time that will also change.

---

for years in order to modify the timing of different cylinders. Before EFI was allowed, NASCAR rules mandated a distributor-triggered ignition; no electronic timing controls could be used. This forces the racers to dig into the distributor to make their own modifications, which is no easy task.

It also limits the use of each modified distributor to certain engines.

For those of us stuck in the real performance world, cylinder-to-cylinder timing can now be accomplished easily through electronic controls. Before you boot up the laptop, let's consider how advanced tuners have controlled cylinder-to-cylinder timing before the advent of personal computers.

Programming

Even though NASCAR's Cup Series has made the switch to EFI with coil-per-cylinder ignitions, the lower classes still use a distributor and CD ignition system. A little cylinder-to-cylinder adjustment may also benefit road racing, off-road, and any higher-RPM, long-endurance application that prohibits the addition of electronic timing controls. Timing has always been a compromise among the cylinders because of variances in the flow of the air/fuel mixture that occurs between combustion chambers, intake tracts, and other variables. For instance, if one or two cylinders run a little lean, the timing will have to be retarded across the board just to compensate for those troubled cylinders.

The only way to advance the ignition timing is to modify the device that triggers the ignition. In the case of distributors, you can zero in on the reluctor or trigger disc inside the distributor. MSD incorporates an eight-paddle reluctor that can be tweaked and moved slightly to advance the trigger signal of specific cylinders. It is important to note that on MSD's baseline Pro-Billet distributor these reluctors are made of a powdered metal; they can be brittle when modifying. The best bet is to use one of its optional billet-steel reluctors. The professional racing HVC distributors are already equipped with the steel reluctor.

The HVC distributor from MSD was developed as a mechanical way to adjust individual cylinder timing. This distributor incorporates dual pickups that are stacked; the

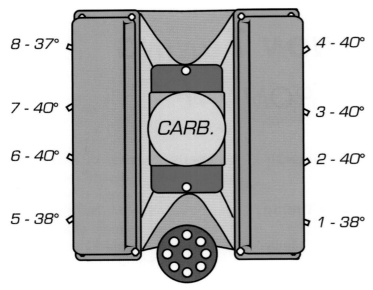

8 - 37°
7 - 40°
6 - 40°
5 - 38°

CARB.

4 - 40°
3 - 40°
2 - 40°
1 - 38°

Each cylinder could benefit from its own specific ignition timing. Due to runner length and engine design, serious engine tuners can make up for some variables, thanks to individual cylinder timing control.

For professional high-RPM, long-endurance racing, MSD offers its HVC line of distributors. These feature stacked magnetic pickups and a billet reluctor that can be machined to compensate for cylinder inefficiencies.

Timing Individual Cylinders Mechanically

Many racing sanctioning bodies do not allow the use of electronic timing devices, and whether they like it or not, racers need to abide by these rules. In certain cases, this promotes a serious amount of reading between the lines, but it can also lead to new product ideas.

Engine builders can go into the distributor to bend or machine the reluctor or paddle in order to alter a cylinder's timing. By slightly repositioning one of the paddles in the direction of its rotation, the timing of that cylinder is advanced. By going against the rotation, the timing is retarded. The trouble is that these paddles weren't meant to be repositioned, so they're easy to break. Moroso, MSD, and Precision Machine offer a billet-steel reluctor that accepts machining and modifying much better than the powdered-metal counterparts that are used in most distributors.

A billet-steel reluctor can be machined to alter each cylinder's timing. This is important in high-end race engines such as those used in stock car racing where electronic controls are not legal. Optically-triggered distributors can also be modified by machining the openings of their trigger discs.

By modifying the window opening of Crane's distributor trigger disc, the timing signal occurs sooner (advanced). Guidelines are even on the disk to assist in your setup. (Photo Courtesy Crane Cams)

secondary pickup (the top one) is adjustable. The pickups are stacked to retain the same cylinder-to-cylinder order when the secondary ignition is selected.

Inside the Crane distributor, a trigger disk is used in conjunction with a light-emitting diode (LED) as the trigger. This trigger disk can be machined to advance when the window opens. It even has guidelines to aid in setting up the distributor. To achieve a retard in certain cylinders, the distributor body must be moved to retard. Then you can compensate other cylinders by machining an advanced position on the disk.

It is important to note that if you switch to the secondary trigger, which is 180 degrees from the primary, the timing will be off. Therefore, on pairs of cylinders, it is best to make timing shifts in the disk.

Once a distributor has been modified, it must always be installed the exact same way with the number-1 cylinder always in the same position. If the cylinder position were moved one terminal over, the entire modified timing map would be off.

Electronic Cylinder Timing

As with most things electronic, it's much easier to tune and adjust cylinder timing through a PC than by physically modifying the distributor. The one challenge you may have with a programmable ignition is setting up a cam synchronization signal. To achieve cylinder-to-cylinder timing, the ignition must know when the number-1 cylinder fires so it can synchronize the custom firing order with the engine's firing order.

A cam sync signal encompasses installation of a distributor with a separate cam-sync pickup, or fabrication of a magnet in the cam gear with a pickup if a belt drive is being used. MSD created an easy way to achieve cam synchronization through the use of an inductive pickup. This device

Using Electronics to Tune Mechanical Distributors

Learning which cylinder to retard or advance takes a lot of engine knowledge, testing, and tuning. One idea for cylinder timing is to run the engine on a dyno or in the car with exhaust gas temperature (EGT) probes in each header tube just outside the cylinder. With testing time, you can quickly identify the best timing per cylinder when the optimum cylinder temperature is achieved. If this procedure is not in your plans, reading the spark plugs and paying attention to your engine and tune-up will point you in the right direction.

When you're modifying a reluctor or trigger wheel to achieve cylinder-to-cylinder timing, it takes a lot of time to learn which cylinder needs what amount of timing for the best results. Even if you have a target retard or advance for each cylinder, you need to make an adjustment, assemble the distributor, run the engine, and then review the data to get it perfect. Then repeat the procedure over and over.

A shortcut is to use one of the ignition controllers on the dyno that provide individual cylinder timing. That way you can monitor and adjust each cylinder through the controller until you achieve the results you're looking for. Once you have this information, you can modify the distributor to meet these requirements and call it good.

To really learn how your engine reacts to individual cylinder timing, you can't beat the dyno. Here you can measure the effects of timing changes with cylinder temperatures and air/fuel values easier with more repeatability than at the track.

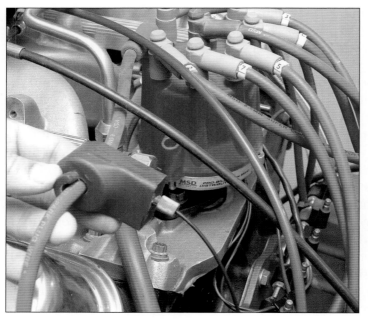

This inductive pickup senses the number-1 cylinder firing so it can begin individual cylinder retards. Even if the cam sync signal is lost during a run, the ignition keeps up with the correct timing order. Once the engine is shut off though, it remains off until the cam sync is repaired.

simply slides over the number-1 plug wire (much like a timing light pickup) and connects to the ignition through a fiber-optic cable. This pickup lets the ignition know when the number-1 cylinder is firing so it can identify and incorporate the individual cylinder retards. In addition, by using the fiber-optic cable, no EMI can interfere with this important signal.

Once the cam sync is set up, you need to go into the ignition and program the cylinders that you want retarded. Be sure you know how to set up the firing order of your specific engine. Where to start? Obviously, time on an engine dyno would be

Another route to achieve a sync signal is with a dual-pickup distributor. This is more prevalent when running an aftermarket EFI system, but it works for cylinder timing as well. In most cases the cam sync pickup is adjustable to phase the signal correctly.

These are screen captures from MSD's Pro-Data+ software showing the individual cylinder timing adjustments (top). The two gauges show timing and RPM in real time. The window marked "Spark-SEQ8" (bottom) shows 1.5 degrees of timing retard for the number-8 cylinder of the firing order being programmed.

the best place to make these adjustments, but if you know your engine and check the plugs constantly, you should have a good idea which cylinders would benefit from a little timing retard.

Remember that any retards programmed for individual cylinder management also need to be taken into consideration for all other programmed retards. For example, all retards are cumulative in the MSD system for a total of 25 degrees. If you pull 4 out of cylinder four, plus 10 on the first nitrous stage, and another 6 going down the track, the total retard is 20 in that cylinder, but only 16 in cylinders with no retard.

All of this talk about PC programming is sort of putting the cart before the horse. Before continuing, let's look at the basics of programmable ignitions and the different uses and options they provide.

Programmable Ignitions

Technology in racing moves as fast as the cars. New controls and ways to make adjustments are constantly developing. It's not uncommon to see racers sitting in their cars with laptops plugged in to review acquired data or make changes to the ECU or controller. Some sanctioning bodies may not like the idea of too much ignition control, but the racers sure seem to like it.

Another benefit to digital technology is being able to combine the most popular timing and RPM accessories into one convenient package. Now you can have a three-step rev limiter, multi-stage retard, a start retard, and an RPM-activated switch

The FireStorm Ignition from Mallory is available in a variety of packages and options. This unit is completely programmable, with controls for ignition and fuel controls.

Notice the serial port connection on the side of the FireStorm? Don't let the amount of wiring overwhelm you. This example offers EFI controls as well as ignition. Moreover, each wire is labeled, making installation much easier.

all in one control, with better control and adjustment through all of them!

The ability to control RPM and timing down to tenths of a degree and RPM in small increments has opened huge tuning opportunities for racers. Just look at the speeds some of the small-tire and drag radial cars are putting down. It has come to the fact that making horsepower is the easy part. The ability to manage all of that power going down the track is what's making it possible to run these incredible numbers.

I'm going to focus on MSD products because they're mandated in several professional race categories and are certainly the majority usage in the pits. That said, many of the features can be accomplished through fuel/ignition management controls and other ignitions as well.

Another note is that you shouldn't be intimidated at all by the features of the software with most of these ignitions. This software probably has more features and adjustments than you'll use, but you'll never race without a laptop again once you spend some time to learn the software and all of the features. All of a sudden you realize that you can program things you didn't think were possible. It's like getting a new video game. The more you play, the better you get.

MSD

The most popular PC programmable ignition control is the MSD Programmable Digital-7 Ignition. Over the years, MSD produced several versions of it and one was mandated in National Hot Rod Association (NHRA) Pro Stock. The units provided a serious spark that could handle the majority of engines and offered some extremely useful programming tools. This ignition has been around for more than 10 years and MSD has since launched its successor, the Power Grid Ignition.

MSD started with a clean slate for the Power Grid, with a lot of input from racers. They developed a completely new software called View and added many new features. As with any computer or software update, many of the same features were retained, but plenty of new toys were

added. Two major design changes were the move to the more common USB port (rather than a bulky old nine-pin serial port) and a smart card for data acquisition.

MSD took a unique approach with Power Grid and made it extremely versatile for use with other ignitions and applications. The Programmable 7 series had five different part numbers to compensate for different features and rules in racing. The Power Grid was divided into two components: the brain and the muscle. The controller (PN 7730) is the brain, and the part that produces the spark only (PN 7720) is the muscle. The "muscle" needs the controller to operate, while the controller is capable of working with a 6AL, a 7AL, or even the Pro-Mag. This means that you can make your existing ignition programmable at a relatively low cost.

The Power Grid controller can also accept different modules, such as a traction-enhancing module, a boost control, and more. This way, MSD doesn't have to offer a new controller for changes in rules or other features.

MSD's Programmable Digital-7 is used in a variety of classes ranging from Pro Stock to Radial Tire classes, as racers take advantage of the programs that fit their needs. To make up for additional features or sanctioning body rules, MSD produced several

The next stage in programming technology from MSD is the Power Grid system. The red box on top is the brain, and the black unit underneath provides a big spark. MSD separated the programming controller so the unit is more versatile and can be used in different applications.

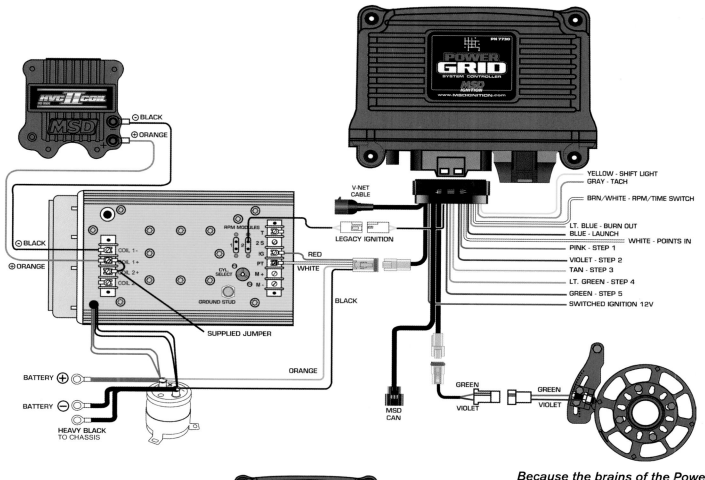

- YELLOW - SHIFT LIGHT
- GRAY - TACH
- BRN/WHITE - RPM/TIME SWITCH
- LT. BLUE - BURN OUT
- BLUE - LAUNCH
- WHITE - POINTS IN
- PINK - STEP 1
- VIOLET - STEP 2
- TAN - STEP 3
- LT. GREEN - STEP 4
- GREEN - STEP 5
- SWITCHED IGNITION 12V

Because the brains of the Power Grid are separated from the ignition, racers can use the control with other ignitions such as the MSD-8 or even a Pro-Mag. At this level of performance, a crank trigger is required.

versions. With the introduction of the Power Grid ignition system, it's reduced the Programmable 7 series, but there are still a lot of them out there. Which one is right for you?

As of this writing, MSD is still producing the PN 7530T that was mandated in NHRA Pro Stock for several years, and the favorite controller simply known as the PN 7531 is still offered. It was the top of the line with all of the bells and whistles, including the launch RPM curve, slew rate rev limiter, and ignition data acquisition.

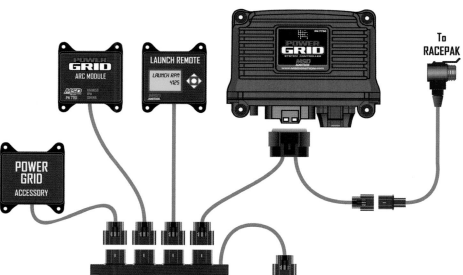

With the Programmable Digital-7 series, MSD offered several units due to rules or programming options. With the Power Grid, there is just one unit and the different accessories are available in plug-in format. Also note the connection to Racepak. The controller provides all of its data to their data acquisition controls.

MSD made five different versions of the Programmable Digital-7 Ignition. Each one had different features, so before you buy a used unit, make sure it's the correct part number and has the features you want.

The Programmable 7-Plus has set the standard for small-tire or drag radial classes thanks to its advanced tuning for RPM and timing controls during the launch, plus a little data acquisition.

If you come across a used one at a great price, be sure it's right for your application. For instance, the PN 7530T for Pro Stock features a traction control detection (TCD) circuit that you don't want to deal with in your outlaw car. The TCD circuit was mandated by NHRA and goes into a rev-limit mode if it senses any manipulation of the trigger signal. It requires a special test tool from NHRA to deactivate. Alternatively, you can leave it powered on for 24 hours straight to cancel the TCD alert.

The original unit, PN 7530, fits most applications but doesn't have the acceleration control (slew rate) feature, boost timing, or data acquisition. You do get a launch-timing curve, gear retards, step retards, and rev limits. In addition, PN 7535 was available; it was just like the original PN 7530 except that it included a boost timing map feature. The PN 75314 is a lesser-known unit that was designed for use on four-cylinder race engines only.

Beware when you're shopping online or at the swap meets as these units are not upgradable to the PN 7531.

Mallory FireStorm

Several other programmable ignitions are available that deliver PC-programmable features. Mallory offers versions of the FireStorm ignition with complete program-

ming options as well as the HyFire VII series.

Electromotive

Electromotive has complete ignition and fuel management systems with the DIS system as well, but we're going to keep our conversation focused on single-channel CD ignition controls at this point.

Holley

We need to tip our hats to Holley when it introduced the Annihilator programmable ignition series in the late 1990s. Unfortunately, the line of ignitions went the way of 6-volt battery systems due to a number of market changes as well as changes within the company. However, Holley's short stint in programmable ignition performance perked up the other companies' efforts.

Timing Retards

Timing requirements in the engine change as the load on the engine changes, such as in different gears and RPM as you race down or around the track. Timing retards can be accomplished in a variety of ways through switches, timers, RPM activation, and so on, but the beauty of the programmable ignition is that you can do nearly anything from the software. From step retards to launch retards, gear retards to cylinder retards, no external switches or controls are needed; just a click of the mouse.

Holeshot Help

One of the most commonly used features in a programmable ignition is to control tire spin to improve 60-foot times. This is hugely beneficial for small-tire and traction-challenged cars. Many racers used

Blurring the Lines

It is an interesting time to be involved in fuel or ignition management. The two systems were always separated from each other. Some companies specialized in ignitions and others handled the fuel side. Today, it's not quite that clear.

Mallory, Accel, MSD, Crane, and others took care of the spark side. The companies that handled fuel injection such as FAST, Holley, and BigStuff3 all made names for themselves with fuel injection systems that allowed racers to control nearly every aspect.

Now it seems that everyone is doing a bit of each. Looking back, Accel was probably the first company to combine the two systems with the DFI fuel injection systems. With the advent of more coil-on-plug systems, fuel system manufacturers don't have to offer a complete line of CD ignitions. Additionally, distributors can have the ability to monitor coil dwell and incorporate OEM crank and cam sensors. Conversely, if an ignition company can control timing and RPM down to fractional increments, what is stopping them from moving into complete controllers?

Currently, the XFI2 system from FAST offers ignition control, as does the Holley Dominator system (and BS3). MSD recently ventured into EFI with the Atomic brand, although at this time it does not have a complete race version with advanced PC tuning capabilities. Electromotive combined its ignition capabilities with fuel controls a number of years ago: If you're looking to kill two birds with one stone, several options are available for controllers with fuel and ignition control integrated.

Things are getting interesting; it's a great time to be a racer!

Different companies divided the ignition and EFI controls into different units. That's not the case today as EFI companies such as Holley and FAST are incorporating ignition-tuning capabilities.

The XFI2 from FAST (top) and the Dominator from Holley (bottom) manage the complete fuel and ignition system. (Photo Courtesy FAST, Holley)

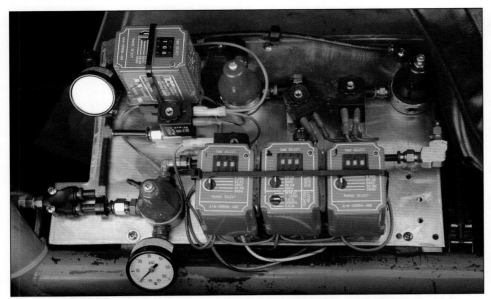

Before programmable ignitions, racers had to incorporate timers to control timing retards or activation of nitrous stages. With the programmable ignition controls and accessories available today, these extra components and wiring are no longer needed.

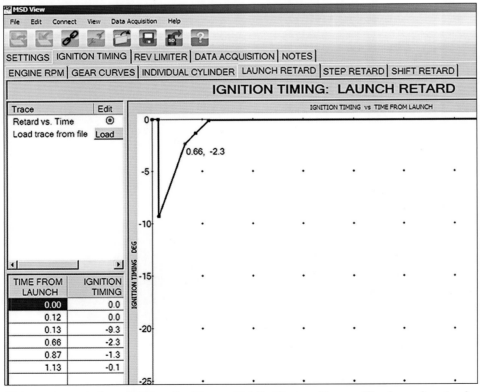

This screen capture is from the Power Grid's View software. The launch retard map starts to retard the timing at .12 second, and by .13 second after the launch the timing is retarded by 9.3 degrees. By just over 1.13 seconds, the timing is brought back to the base setting, as shown in the lower left of the screen.

to wire in a timer to activate a timing control to retard the timing. A programmable ignition replaces all of those components and allows you to control the timing at the launch. By retarding the timing at the hit, it softens the power of the engine and by tuning; the goal is to balance the power with what the track will hold.

Programmable ignitions accomplish this is in a variety of ways. You can select a timing retard that activates when the launch button is released and ramp the timing back over a period of time. For example, as soon as the car launches, you can retard the timing 10 degrees for .8 second. The nice thing is that the timing is ramped in over that .8-second window for a smooth transition back to the base timing setting. This ramp, or transition period, prevents the timing from "snapping" back to the base timing and is easier on the engine and driveline.

Another option to set a timing retard is through a timing map with which it's possible to plot a timing curve based on timing and RPM. The PN 7531 and the Power Grid offer the ability to build a timing map for each gear.

Time-Based Rev Limit

One adjustment that is much more user friendly that assists with holeshot consistency is the time-based rev limit of the PN 7531. This map lets you program an RPM curve, much like a timing curve. However, instead of basing timing on RPM, you set an RPM limit for every second or less.

The best way to program this map is by making a good pass and using that data file as a basis for a starting point. You can add RPM points for every .1 second so a map can easily be plotted. When the RPM reaches over the set point, cylinders are dropped to keep the RPM at the rate programmed. This is a great way to prevent the tires from spinning. It can be extremely helpful when programmed correctly.

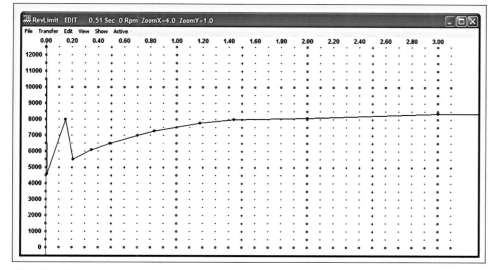

The Rev Limit chart of the PN 7531 is a time-based RPM limit that you can map in 100-rpm increments every .1 second. Talk about help in getting small-tire and radial cars launched! In this example, when the car launches, the timer starts and the RPM limit follows the line you program.

Gear Curves

In racing applications, the timing requirements in first gear are much different than the engine's needs in high gear. Maybe you're shifting into fourth as you hit a rough spot on the track at about 900 feet. Today's programmable ignitions allow you to map a timing curve or set a timing change for each gear. But how does the ignition recognize what gear you're in?

When the transmission shifts, the RPM drops. When an ignition senses that drop, it counts it as a gear change and moves to any programs that are set for that gear (such as a timing map, shift light, etc.). Because every engine combination is different, you can program the gear change RPM drop to match your application. It can be set closer (less RPM change) for high-winding, close-ratio setups,

Holeshot Timing Curve

As mentioned above, taking timing out of the engine during the holeshot helps control tire spin by incorporating a timer and a retard step. MSD's Programmable Ignition has this feature built in and takes it to another level.

This controller has a holeshot retard program that lets you select a retard amount that is activated as soon as the car launches. This is done through a control wire spliced into the trans-brake or clutch switch. Once you determine how much timing you wish to retard, you can also set the amount of time that the ignition timing takes to ramp back up to the total.

This is an example of a retard curve used during launch. The timing retard begins to ramp back to the set timing as soon as the car launches. In order to soften the hit to the tires, you adjust the amount of retard and the amount of time it takes to ramp back.

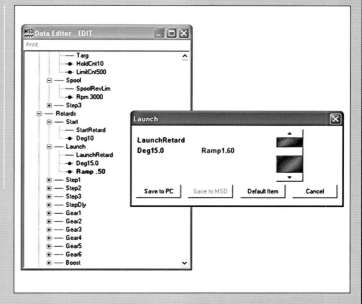

or to a much bigger RPM change to suit your combination. This provides the ability to really dial in your car for specific tracks or applications.

First gear requires a much different timing map than fourth or fifth gear. In fact, in first gear you may be retarding the timing to help soften the initial shock to the slicks, and then want all the timing back in when you shift into second. This is similar to setting the mechanical advance in a distributor, but now you can modify it to handle gear change torque peaks, tire shake at certain points, or even to add a little timing at a certain RPM. Advancing the timing is possible on almost any timing control, but you have to reset the total timing by moving the crank trigger pickup to the advanced position. Remember, an ignition has no way of advancing the timing, it only knows what the pickup tells it!

Once the overall timing is advanced, you have to compensate for the advance at the crank trigger in each timing curve and any other retard rates you program. Having the timing a little advanced gives you the opportunity to make very quick and very accurate timing changes through the program, rather than repositioning the pickup.

Gear Maps

Before you program timing maps for each gear, you select the number of gears for your car. Then you go to the gear retard graph and plot out what you want to accomplish in each gear. If you don't plan to change the curve for any gears, you still need to copy and paste the curve for each gear. This derived from racers needing a first-gear-only curve (to help them get off the line and rolling). The middle gears are fairly constant, but some of the restricted high-performance racers wanted to put a little timing back into the engine at high RPM to get a little torque back in the engine.

Boost Timing Map

As if there weren't enough timing maps for tuning, there's also a chart you can program based on boost/vacuum pressure. Of course a manifold absolute pressure (MAP) sensor is required to operate in supercharged or turbocharged applications. This feature provides the opportunity to retard timing as boost pressure increases to prevent engine-damaging detonation and pre-ignition. The amount of adjustment varies depending on the MAP sensor you select.

Step Retard

Some step retards can be based on nitrous stage activation or RPM. These retards all have activation wires that need to be connected to a 12-volt signal to activate them. The Power Grid has five step retards versus four of the Programmable 7 series.

One advantage of programmable step retards is that you can ramp each retard step on or off from its full retard amount. For example, when the third stage turns on for 6 degrees, you could have it ramp from zero retard to 6 degrees over the course of .2 second and even ramp the timing back in over time. This setup is good for racers who want a change for each gear rather than cumulating each step. On the other hand, you can activate each retard stage by a specific RPM.

Another nifty feature is that you can delay the amount of time for a retard to turn off after the 12-volt signal is removed from its activation wire. This is handy when using nitrous, as the timing retard is in effect for a set amount of time to clear any remaining traces of the gas from the engine before the timing

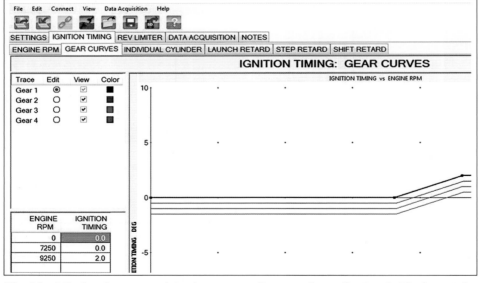

The ideal timing for an engine changes as it races down the track. Timing at the top end is much different than during first and second gear. Using a programmable ignition allows you to map a curve for each gear. This chart shows a 4-speed transmission with four timing maps spaced .5 degree apart from each other.

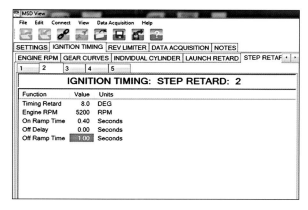

Programmable ignitions provide additional control over a basic step retard as well. In this case, step two is set to retard the timing 8 degrees when the engine reaches over 5,200 rpm. The retard ramps down within .4 second and when deactivated the timing slowly ramps back in over a 1-second range.

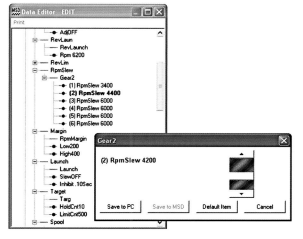

The often overly hyped and confused slew-rate rev limiter in MSD's systems allows you to select a rate of acceleration limiter for each gear. It is easy to set with a couple mouse taps, but grasping what is best for your car comes through testing and reviewing data files of each pass.

goes back to total time. This can be adjusted in small increments under 2.5 seconds.

RPM Function

As mentioned earlier, the engine load changes as you race down the track, and so can the shift points. These ignitions let you program a different RPM for each gear to activate a shift light. This can also be helpful if you need to short shift a couple gears, as the light can be made to come on exactly when you need to shift. An RPM-activated window switch in the control lets you activate an accessory at a selected RPM and turn it off at a different RPM. You can also activate a circuit based on RPM, boost, or even time on certain models.

Slew Limit

The slew-rate rev limiter was probably one of the most talked-about and misunderstood MSD programs.

"Slew" refers to an RPM-to-time ratio that you select to control the engine's rate of acceleration. This means that if you select 1,000 rpm per second for the slew rate, it takes your engine 5 seconds to reach 5,000 rpm (1,000 rpm rate of acceleration per second).

With the PN 7531 you can select a different slew limit for each gear, from 100 to 9,900 rpm per second. Any RPM setting is based on 1 second and the time is not adjustable. This ratio gives you an entirely new window for tuning and is a fresh way of controlling tire spin going down the track.

To successfully use the slew limit, the ideal situation is to determine your engine's rate of acceleration in each gear. This is best determined through data logging and reviewing the information from several good runs. The PN 7531 and the Power Grid have ignition data recording capabilities that you can review and save on your laptop. By finding the ideal rate of acceleration, you can ensure that the tires stay planted, because if the engine starts to accelerate too quickly, the rev limiter is activated to maintain the slew setting.

Setting the slew rate isn't as simple as it sounds. You need to have several ideal passes under your belt to provide good useable information. Moreover, every car and engine is different and reacts differently going down the track. To make up for these variances, MSD programmed a couple of different settings into the slew program. These include a target variance in RPM, and a high and low margin to compensate for crankshaft flexing and sharp timing variances between firings.

ARC Module

The Power Grid doesn't have a built-in RPM control like the slew-rate limit but has an even more advanced (add-on) version called the Advanced RPM Control (ARC) module. The ARC module is as close to traction control that you can get, without having an active control that learns and makes adjustments on the fly. You still have to program the ARC, and if you program it incorrectly, chances are you'll slow down!

The ARC has several advanced features that racers wanted. You can base your rev limit, timing, or acceleration on crankshaft RPM or use a driveshaft sensor to map a timing

RPM map. You'd be amazed at the difference between the two values.

Nitrous racers also wanted to be able to use this feature, but without the rev-limiting function. The ARC provides a way to pull out timing to try to maintain traction rather than bumping up on the rev limiter as well. The Power Grid and ARC Module give you a variety of ways to save a bad run.

The Power Grid doesn't have every available feature built into it. This was done on purpose to keep the control legal in different race series. If a racer wants to run a boost retard or control the RPM during acceleration, a plug-in module is required.

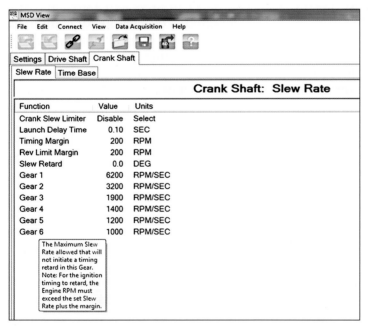

The ARC module of the Power Grid provides the slew rate and timing control features. This version, when compared to the original (PN 7531), offers different settings for the crankshaft RPM or driveshaft RPM.

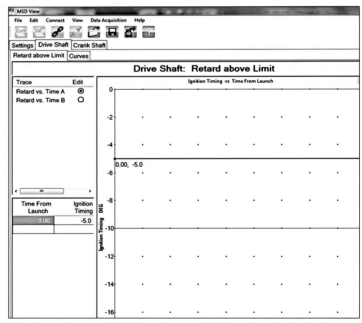

This example shows a racer programming a timing limit in the ARC settings. When the crankshaft RPM exceeds the programmed limit the system pulls out 5 degrees of timing to help reduce the power and, therefore, wheel speed.

EFI and Ignition Controllers

When you get into EFI systems you are in another realm of tuning possibilities with fuel maps, RPM, ignition, and more. Several of these systems integrate ignition system outputs and calibrations.

The inductive distributorless gurus at Electromotive have been providing EFI systems for years and now offer a complete system that incorporates the HPX coil-pack ignition system. These systems, called the Total Engine Control 3 (TEC3), are available for a variety of engine platforms and applications.

The TEC3 is programmable through the Windows-based WinTEC software, complete with easy-to-follow pull-down menus and clear screens that are easy to navigate and tune. This EFI/ignition system has data-acquisition capabilities that allow you to overlay screens and graphs to compare different passes.

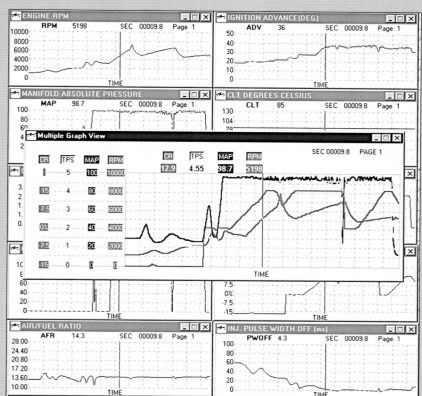

Electromotive's software has a Tuning Wizard that gets the engine fired up with minimal inputs. Then you can tune the engine on the fly to get it dialed in with a number of inputs and options. (Photo Courtesy Electromotive, Inc.)

Electromotive offers complete EFI systems that include their accurate and high-output DIS ignition system. The TEC3 system gives you an infinite number of areas to tune for the most performance. (Photo Courtesy Electromotive, Inc.)

GOING DIS
WHERE'S THE DISTRIBUTOR?

The distributor, as we know it, is extinct when it comes to new vehicles. The extinction process started slowly on a few cars from the early 1980s, and it really became apparent to performance enthusiasts on the turbo V-6 engines of the Grand National and T-Type Buicks. The trend continued gaining momentum, and when Chevrolet put the distributor behind the water pump on the LT-1 engines in 1993/1994 models, it was a sign that the distributor was on its last legs. Just a few years later (with the introduction of the LS platform) they were gone.

For Blue Oval fans, the introduction of the Modular motor brought two coil packs to the front of the engine instead of the familiar TFI distributor. Those coil packs still incorporated spark plug wires, as did the newer Hemi coil packs, but each only lasted a few more years. The next generation of ignition systems for these Ford and Chrysler engines ditched the wires and moved to coil-on-plug technology; no distributor and no wires to be concerned about. Even though there aren't any new engines using distributors these days, there are still plenty of distributors out on the street.

Today, any newer engine is equipped with a coil-per-cylinder ignition system. If you have an eight-cylinder engine, you will have eight coils, four coils for four-cylinder engines, and so on. This doesn't seem like a money-saving upgrade for the big guys because they're now buying several times as many coils as before. However, they also don't have to plan around a bulky, inefficient distributor, plus they have much better control over each cylinder's timing. The

This is an over-the-top example of a high-performance solution to a distributor-less ignition system. This Ford Modular engine is all about horsepower with the blower, and to ensure combustion under extreme boost, eight MSD Pro Power HVC II coils are driven through an eight-channel ECU.

Chrysler combined coil-on-plug with coil-near-plug technology for the reintroduction of their twin spark plug Hemi engine. These coils are part of a waste-spark system, but use a spark plug wire to go to a different cylinder. Later models use a version without the spark plug wire. This example is on a late-model Hemi engine that is being retrofit with a carburetor.

When General Motors first did away with the decades-old, rear-mounted distributor, they moved it to the front of the engine right behind the water pump. This engine platform was introduced in the early to mid-1990s as the LT1 and the "pancake" distributor was called an Opti-Spark. This engine now has a cult following and will always be compared to the latest LT1 (that is, based on the direct-injection LS platform).

coils are much smaller because they only fire one time for every complete engine cycle. There is plenty of time to charge each coil, and that results in a hotter spark through higher RPM. All this adds up to improved performance and economy, which is exactly why you're seeing more of these systems.

What does this mean for performance enthusiasts? There are more electronics involved with distributorless ignition systems (DIS), but performance ignition components are available for many of them. In addition, as the aftermarket catches up to the OEMs, we will see better controls and adjustments for ignition timing and RPM control.

Technological Advances

A distributor shaft spins thanks to the helically cut gears that connect it to the camshaft. One of these gears is integral to the camshaft.

This is rotated through another set of gears that are joined by a chain to the crankshaft. It's a long procession of mechanical meshing and turning, which means that there are

Ford has been using a coil-on-plug design since 2004. These compact coils fit right over the spark plug so no secondary wire is necessary. High-output aftermarket models are available from sources such as Accel, MSD, and Granatelli Motorsports.

inevitable inefficiencies. Now, put all of these components under the load of full throttle. Any variables that were minute at idle or moderate speeds now become a significant factor. The mechanical flexing and twisting, varying frequencies, harmonics, and the pistons pounding down on the crank can all add up to timing variations.

As engine component technology has progressed, the RPM that race engines run and live through has also escalated. These extra RPM have brought out slight timing gremlins that didn't necessarily come into play a few years ago. High RPM brings out the worst in a distributor that is responsible for triggering the ignition. This is one reason that most high-end racecars trigger the ignition with a crank trigger system. It was within the last few years that Top Fuel dragsters and even sprint cars incorporated crank triggers to fire their magnetos. This brought awesome results in timing accuracy compared to having the trigger inside the generator. It wasn't really a fault in the distributor that brought about its demise; it was electronics and ensuing technology. The demise of the distributor wasn't instant. Signs

were obvious over the years as OEMs incorporated more electronics and controllers. At one point in the mid-1980s, the popular GM HEI distributor lost its entire centrifugal advance assembly in favor of maintenance-free (and more accurate) electronic control of the spark advance. Ford also backed away from mechanical weights and springs at the same time with its TFI distributors.

The next nail in the coffin was stripping away the distributor's responsibility to supply trigger signals. Using a sensor on the crankshaft provided a much more accurate signal. This left the distributor simply distributing the sparks from the all-new electronic ignition system.

Because the ignition was fired from a crank sensor and the advanced electronics in the ignition module controlled the dwell and spark delivery, it certainly made sense to do away with the distributor completely. This was accomplished by incorporating multiple coil packs to increase the voltage and distribute

it to the spark plugs. Welcome to distributorless ignition technology.

Early DIS Development

One of the first late-model muscle engines to go distributorless was the Buick turbo V-6. This engine used a single coil-pack assembly that consisted of three dual-tower coil packs. As performance fans increased the boost and power of the V-6, the need for a powerful ignition emerged. This posed quite a challenge to ignition companies that were used to a single-channel distributor.

Accel and MSD introduced a four-channel CD ignition, but the wiring could be a daunting task. It's almost like wiring three separate ignition systems. MSD developed an interface module for the sought-after intercooled 1986 and 1987 models that sandwiched between the coil packs and the ignition module. It connects the coils directly to the DIS-4 unit.

A number of different versions of DIS ignitions are available, although they are similar in their function.

Going DIS means there are no more caps and rotors to wear or replace. Early systems incorporated spark plug wires, but now some factory systems put the coil right on top of the spark plug. This coil pack and module assembly is on a 1986 Buick Grand National, one of the first modern muscle cars to use DIS technology.

These are factory LS coils. Over the developmental lifespan of the engine, General Motors has used at least five different coils with changes in the connector or housing. Even with their compact design these coils are quite robust.

HIGH-PERFORMANCE IGNITION SYSTEMS

Some systems have coil packs that fire two cylinders at once. One cylinder is under compression, while its opposite cylinder is on the exhaust stroke. This design is referred to as a waste-spark system. You'd think that it would take away from the coil's output by firing two cylinders, but remember that one cylinder is on the exhaust stroke, so there is no cylinder pressure. This means that it doesn't take much voltage to jump the plug gap. Even though two cylinders are getting fired, the coil pack and the spark still have plenty of punch.

Coil Pack Ignition Upgrades

Coil pack DIS ignition technology has been available for more than 20 years, and most companies in the aftermarket offer a variety of components and accessories. Most waste-spark coil pack applications used a coil with two or four secondary towers. GM used dual-tower coils for many years, while Ford introduced four-tower coils when it moved to the Modular Motor (for the first few years).

With these types of systems, the aftermarket could still easily access the coil negative wire that served as the trigger wire from the ECU. By intercepting this signal, and being able to access the positive and negative coil terminals, the aftermarket was able to offer a multiple-spark CD ignition, similar to a 6AL, although it had multiple channels. An example is MSD's DIS-4 Ignition Control, which has four channels (similar to

having four 6ALs in one) and could fire four coil packs for eight-cylinder operation. Some CD ignitions were also available as a DIS-2 designed for four-cylinder engines.

The installation of these units is similar to that of a single-channel, distributor-triggered ignition. Two sets of coil primary wires (outputs) and two input wires intercept the ECU's trigger signal. The supply wires connect to the battery positive and

The MSD DIS-4 Ignition Control is a four-channel CD ignition, meaning it can fire four waste-spark dual-tower coil packs (or two four-towers). A two-channel (DIS-2) version is available for four-cylinder engines. Neither of these controls can be used for coil-on-plug applications.

General Motors has used these two-tower coil packs since the mid-1980s to fire many of their four- and six-cylinder engines. Most ignition companies offer replacement performance models for this style of coil.

Advanced ignition technology meets traditional Hemi muscle. These two coil packs have four towers each and are set up as a waste-spark system. This means two towers fire at the same time, while one cylinder is on the compression stroke and the other is on the exhaust stroke.

negative terminals and one on/off wire. The installation is not complicated, but can be challenging.

It is highly recommended to have the wiring diagram for your vehicle so you know for sure what color wire does what function. Similar to distributor-fired ignitions, the factory tach and the EFI may need a tach adapter (or possibly two) to function properly.

The DIS-4 unit can also be used on six-cylinder engines with three coil packs. These ignitions fit most engines that use coil packs in waste-spark systems. They're not intended for ignitions with a single coil per cylinder, although I've seen it a couple times on engines whose electrical systems had been modified.

When Ford moved to individual coil packs, MSD offered a kit that consisted of two DIS-4 ignitions, four tach adapters, and a wiring harness. The system functioned, delivering high-output sparks combined with a two-step and retard stage. However, the wiring (and the price) weren't for the faint of heart.

If you're looking for improved coil output with a waste-spark system, you can create your own by wiring two high-output coils together in series so the system still has its waste-spark capabilities. This is accomplished by connecting a wire between the coil's negative terminal to the other coil's positive terminal. The ignition's primary wires for that channel go to the first coil's positive post and the negative wire to the second coil's negative terminal. By tying two Accel, MSD, or Crane performance coils together, you can get a higher voltage for your waste-spark system.

Late-Model Muscle

It is difficult to install a CD ignition on a late-model distributorless system. The question also arises as to whether a CD spark is even necessary to boost power in the first place. Remember, with eight coils, quite a lot of time is available for each coil to charge up to capacity compared to a distributor with a single coil. Moreover, coil technology has improved so much that efficient, powerful coils are coming from the OEM as well as the aftermarket. I've seen LS engines produce well over 1,000 horsepower while using factory coils.

GM's LS coils make it a challenge to install an aftermarket CD ignition. Inside each coil is a compact driver circuit that monitors the dwell and controls each coil, which is why they've earned the nickname "smart" coils. Mallory's FireStorm ignition system, for example, is designed for the LS platform with the proper connections for the various cam and crank sensors of the different engines. Their race kits, however, require the FireStorm CD coil and are not designed to run with factory EFI systems. The FireStorm system is really for race or complete retro-fit applications and provides a lot of output and tuning control.

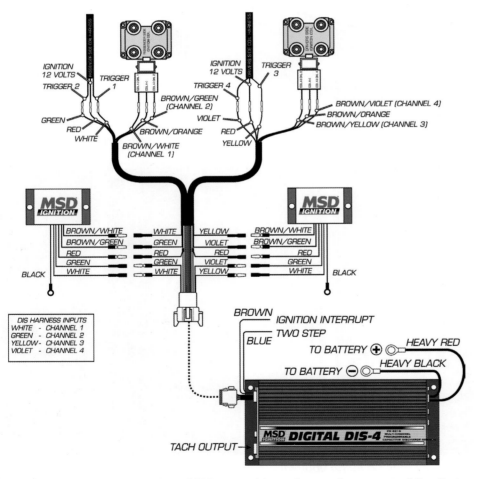

The Digital DIS-4 ignition from MSD was able to fire up the output of the first-generation Ford Modular Motor when they ran two coil packs with waste-spark technology. These engines also required two special tach adapters.

Accel offers performance upgrade coils for all GM LS models. These coils are designed to produce 10 to 15 percent more energy than the OEM version and mount in the same position with matching connectors. (Photo Courtesy Accel Ignition)

MSD, Accel, Granatelli Motorsports, and other companies offer LS coils with improved output in a factory-style housing. In Chapter 5 I discuss how engineers can sap increased spark energy from coils by manipulating the turns ratio and materials. That can still be done with LS coil designs.

MSD's LS coils produce multiple sparks during cranking and low RPM to promote quick starts and throttle response. Because the LS coils are mounted close to, but not on, the spark plug (sometimes referred to as coil-near-plug), they still require a spark plug wire to transfer the voltage from the coil to the plug. As in most cases, the factory parts are made to be adequate. Many spark plug wires with lower resistance are available to use on LS engines.

Ford and Chrysler use coil-on-plug technology, so spark plug wires aren't needed at all. These small "pencil" coils typically fit in a sleeve or tube from the top of the cylinder head that reaches to the plug. The design is incredibly efficient but the confined space limits coil capacity. Of

When an aftermarket ECU is incorporated, you can choose what coils work best for your application. This land speed racer uses eight of MSD's compact Blaster SS coils because of their performance, size, and ease of mounting. A MoTech engine controller manages the spark and timing.

MSD designed a replacement coil for three different LS coils that have been used over the engine's lifespan. These coils have increased spark energy and even produce multiple sparks during cranking and low RPM. General Motors used several different versions of the coil, so make sure you know which style your coil brackets require.

RPM and Timing Control Challenges

If you're looking for timing control, a two-step rev limiter, or boost-timing curve, MSD offers a line of controls that give you the tuning opportunity. The 6LS and 6-Hemi connect to factory connectors and allow you to program certain ignition aspects from your laptop, all while working in conjunction with the factory EFI system.

The Windows-based Pro-Data Plus software provides a timing map, RPM controls, and other items. These controls require a lot of wiring and provide the desired results. However, tuners that connect through the diagnostic port of late-model vehicles render many common ignition accessories obsolete. It is interesting to note that these controls are more popular for late-model engines installed in older cars and topped with a carburetor.

Mallory introduced an all-new programmable ignition series called the FireStorm. A number of different applications are available for the advanced ignition, from single-channel CD designs to multi-channel LS ignition kits.

Granatelli Motorsports offers improved output coils for late-model muscle cars. The coils produce higher voltage and recover more efficiently at high RPM to aid the combustion process at modified and higher RPM.

The 6-Hemi Controller drives the coil packs and controls the timing on engines that have been retrofit to a carburetor. With the addition of a wiring harness, they also support timing and RPM changes with the factory EFI.

This cutaway of a pencil coil shows the windings packed in a small space. This is a challenge to the aftermarket because space is limited. Engineers can modify the spark output and profile with different winding ratios and materials, but it's tough in such a small package.

For LS racers, Lingenfelter Performance also offers an adjustable launch control. Setting a lower launch RPM helps produce consistent launches.

MSD offers the 2 Step Launch Controls for GM LS engines as well as the Ford Mod Motor and Coyote platform. The units wire into the OEM wiring and have simple rotary dial settings on the side of the unit that set the launch RPM.

course, that doesn't stop the aftermarket, and a variety of coils are available for the Ford Coyote and Mod Motor as well as the late-model Hemi.

The positive side is that these coils are not smart coils, which keeps replacement costs lower because no electronic circuitry is built into the coils. In addition, you could run a different coil with an aftermarket eight-channel DIS ignition or EFI system in an exotic racing application. Systems from Holley, FAST, and BigStuff3 have fuel control as well as ignition control features and programs for eight-channel ignition systems.

NASCAR's premier Sprint Cup series was recently in the limelight for its mandate of EFI. When it moved to EFI, coil-per-cylinder ignition systems were also incorporated, much to the chagrin of distributor and ignition manufacturers. The ignition system is controlled through the ECU; at this time no external CD ignition accessories are allowed (or available). It is doubtful they will become available in the future due to the extra wiring and price that would be attached. The teams already have control over the charge time and ignition timing of each cylinder through the same ECU that controls fuel injection.

Launch Control

If modern performance cars have any downside, it has to be the advanced electronic controls that you can't access and the difficulty of adding accessories. That may be more of a challenge for aftermarket companies than for the enthusiast because the aftermarket has to come up with components for traditional applications that racers want or are used to having.

One seemingly simple item that drag racers like is a two-step RPM limit. Having a lower RPM limit that can be switched on at the starting line helps keep the engine at a consistent launch RPM and gives the racer the ability to focus on cutting a respectable reaction time rather than watching the tach. There are a couple ways to get this.

Putting a carburetor on a newer LS engine is becoming popular and is carrying over to the new Hemi engines and, to a lesser extent, the Ford Modular. To drive the coils, an ignition control is necessary. MSD offers versions for these engines and Edelbrock offers one with their LS intake system.

Even new-style Hemis are being adapted to use an old-school fuel system. Even though a carb is feeding the air and fuel, there is still no distributor so you need a special control to drive the coil-on-plug system.

Lingenfelter Performance and MSD offer add-on two-steps, or launch controls. The units are designed to wire into the engine before the coils receive the trigger signals. To activate the lower-RPM limit an activation wire can be toggled from a momentary switch, through the clutch switch, or even a transbrake. When activated, the RPM holds at a set limit. As soon as the button is released, the RPM go screaming up to get down the track.

Carburetors versus EFI

Modern engines are models of great engineering. They are smaller and lighter, yet make more power than their predecessors of the muscle car age. You're starting to see a lot more of these engines being retrofit into street rods and muscle cars. The one hurdle that has made people refrain from taking advantage of late-model performance for their classic car is the thought of trying to figure out the EFI system. Now there's an easy way to get over that hurdle and rip down the home stretch: install a carburetor.

That's right, the venerable old carburetor is being installed on LS2s, new Hemis, and even on overhead-cam Modular Ford engines. This eases the installation because you don't need to mount and wire an ECU or fab up an in-tank pump. What about the ignition? These engines aren't designed to accept a distributor.

MSD offers a 6-LS ignition controller, designed to drive the factory coils of a GM LS-based engine. The controller connects to the OEM crank sensor, cam sensor, MAP sensor, and coolant temperature sensor. Is also connects to the factory coils mounted on top of the valve covers.

The ignition timing can be controlled through plug-in timing curve modules or via a PC. When connected through a PC, other programs can be set such as a two-step rev limit, nitrous retard, or even a boost map for forced induction. Edelbrock and GMPP offer similar controls with their intake manifolds for the LS engines. For Ford and Chrysler fans, similar controls are available to handle the spark when a

Distributors for LS Engines?

Leave it to hot rodders and racers to adapt old-school technology to modern engine performance. First, they did it by offering intake manifolds that adapt a carburetor to an LS or Hemi engine (and a few Mod Motors). The next step took a lot of work.

GM Performance Parts first introduced a complete front-drive accessory system that provided the ability to run a distributor off the front of the cam. That's right, you can run a distributor on an LS engine. The system works great and keeps things easy for enthusiasts who don't want to adapt, but it makes your GM engine look like a Ford. In fact, the front assembly requires a Ford 302 distributor.

Another application is based on class rules and components. Racing Head Services and its parent company, Comp Cams, offer a front-drive kit for GM LSX blocks as well as the RHS LS-based block that has a provision for an MSD 12LT Pro-Mag.

As the LS engine gains more acceptance in circle-track applications, this style of front drive will allow racers to run an LS with a magneto. These race-specific systems have provisions for Sprint-car-style oil pumps and water pumps with integrated AN-fitting adapters and even integral cam and crank sensors.

A distributor or magneto mounted to the front of an LS engine? Comp Cams teamed up with Racing Head Services to design a drive assembly specifically for Sprint cars so they could take advantage of the LS engine architecture.

GMPP offers a kit that accepts a Ford (gasp!) distributor to trigger and control the spark timing of an LS engine. By using a distributor and carburetor you can take advantage of late-model technology without venturing into EFI, multiple coils, and PC programming territory. (Photo Courtesy GM Performance Parts)

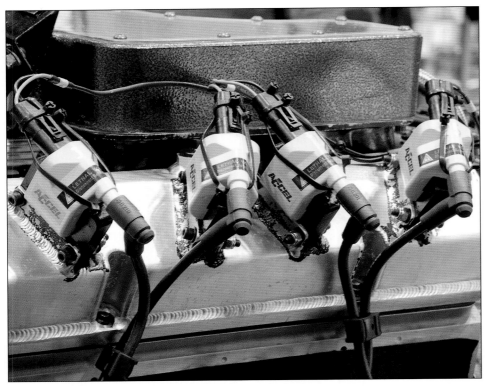

These Accel coils are being used in a race application with an advanced EFI management system handling both the fuel and ignition side of things. This is what the future holds for racing on many fronts.

Many folks don't like the look of an LS engine with the coils mounted on top of the valve covers. Holley Performance offers several coil covers that give the engine more of a big-block look, especially in the case where a carb or throttle body is used with a factory air cleaner topping the system.

carburetor is being used on a Mod Motor or 5.7L Hemi.

Retrofit Ignitions

All of this distributorless ignition technology sounds pretty convincing, but you've got a lot invested in a big-block Chevy or 426 Hemi. Is there a way to reap the benefits of late-model technology on these classic engines? Of course there is! Companies such as Electromotive and Compu-Tronix offer ignition kits to make the move to distributorless performance.

Electromotive

Electromotive has been using coil pack technology for many years and offers two kits and several complete operating systems with EFI and ignition controls. In fact, the company holds several important patents in connection with DIS operation and coil charging.

With one coil for every two cylinders, the charge time of each coil can be four times that of a distributor-triggered ignition. This means that the ignition has no trouble producing full-output sparks to well over racing RPM. In addition, the spark duration is extended thanks to the inductive firing characteristics (see Chapter 4).

The Electromotive XDI system is easy to install on most traditional engines with a distributor. If you are lacking firewall clearance or you simply want to get away from the gear-driven trigger mechanism and delivery of a distributor, Electromotive makes it easy for you.

Its system uses a crank trigger to provide the XDI with trigger information. Unlike crank trigger systems, the XDI uses a wheel with 58 teeth

Electromotive has systems that use rotary dials rather than requiring a PC for timing adjustments. This unit has adjustments for initial and advanced timing as well as RPM settings. (Photo Courtesy Electromotive, Inc.)

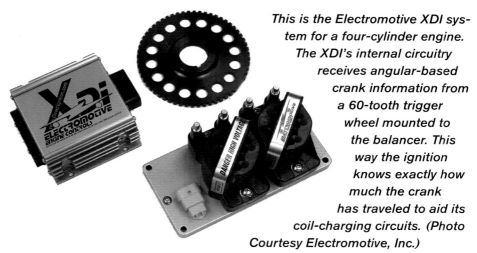

This is the Electromotive XDI system for a four-cylinder engine. The XDI's internal circuitry receives angular-based crank information from a 60-tooth trigger wheel mounted to the balancer. This way the ignition knows exactly how much the crank has traveled to aid its coil-charging circuits. (Photo Courtesy Electromotive, Inc.)

and a magnetic pickup. The extra teeth provide more information so the ignition knows the location and angle of the crankshaft throughout every revolution. This means that the XDI can make firing and rev-limiting compensations, and this aids in precision charging of each coil pack.

The XDI system keeps things simple with rotary dial adjustments to compensate for rev limits. The XDI2 delivers the same PC programming that supports their complete EFI system, but only on the ignition side. This includes a three-dimensional load and RPM-based ignition table, knock sensor, two-step RPM controls, and advanced launch controls. A drag race box also offers an RPM window switch and multiple retard steps.

The greatest benefit to an inductive system is spark duration. With a coil pack ignition system such as the XDI, an inductive system has time to charge each coil pack between firings so you can take advantage of the lengthy duration. Electromotive offers performance enthusiasts a different way to think about ignition systems and inductive ignitions in

The Electromotive system incorporates a slim, multi-tooth trigger wheel that supplies the ignition trigger signal through a pickup from the crankshaft. This provides rock-steady ignition timing and the capability for precision tuning. (Photo Courtesy Electromotive, Inc.)

The XDI2 system forgoes the rotary dials for programming in favor of laptop programming. Electromotive basically stripped out the ignition side of their engine management software and offers ignition-only features in the XDI2 system. (Photo Courtesy Electromotive, Inc.)

Compu-Tronix provides a solution to go distributorless. The inductive ignition system comes with a distributor plug that provides a trigger signal to fire two four-tower coil packs. The system increases spark energy and provides improved dwell control to enhance performance. (Photo Courtesy Compu-Tronix)

These are all examples of modern DIS coils. Some still require spark plug wires, but their days could also be numbered. There are no wires on many sport compacts these days, nor on Ford Modulars or the latest Hemi. Plug wires could be going the same way as the distributor.

The pseudo distributor from Compu-Tronix mounts low in the block and answers the need for the oil pump. The unit connects to the two coil packs, providing a simple and effective opportunity to retrofit DIS technology to an older engine. (Photo Courtesy Compu-Tronix)

particular. It offers a variety of different trigger wheels and accessories to make installing an XDI easy with only a few wires to connect. The one thing you need to buy separately is a new set of plug wires.

Compu-Tronix

The Compu-Tronix Performance Ignition Systems also use coil packs with a waste spark. However, rather than having to install a trigger wheel on the crankshaft, it has a unique way of triggering the ignition.

Compu-Tronix incorporates a distributor "plug" that triggers the coil packs. These plugs mount in place of the distributor but are low-profile sealed components so they offer a solution to limited firewall clearance. Because they mount in place of the distributor, there are no

challenges to installing a crankshaft trigger wheel that might have caused issues with pulley alignment.

Inside the distributor plug is a pickup that triggers each coil pack. Their system for V-8 engines is called the DIS8 and they offer other systems for VW Type 1 engines and several Porsche powerplants. The domestic V-8 kits are complete with distributor trigger system, coil packs, and wiring. No programming controls or PCs are required; simply bolt it in and never worry about changing a distributor cap and rotor again.

Summary

These are just a couple examples of distributorless ignition systems, and you can bet that more are coming. As enthusiasts become comfortable with all those coils and the

programming, you'll see more coil-per-cylinder systems at the track and on the street.

Some companies (such as Electromotive) are intertwining their advanced ignition-controlling technology with their own fuel-injection systems. Other companies are adding more ignition programming features and drivers for coil packs to their EFI-controlling systems. MoTeC and FAST are known for their EFI programming capabilities on race engines around the world, and they have been adding more ignition tuning functions and spark controls to their ECU controllers.

One thing is for certain: distributorless ignitions are not going away anytime soon. It's the distributor that is going away, and coil-per-cylinder is here to stay.

BATTERIES, CHARGING AND WIRING
FUEL FOR THE FIRE

I've covered all the parts and components necessary to produce a high-performance ignition system. There is, however, one other system on your car that dictates how the ignition performs: the charging system. This system includes the battery that provides a reserve of voltage and current primarily to start the engine, and the alternator that continuously creates the current needed for the electrical components.

Battery

The battery of your car is like a fuel tank full of electricity. It gets the car running by powering the starter and ignition, and other components such as the fuel pump and EFI system. Once the engine fires up, the charging system takes over the supply chores (and fills the battery to capacity again). Unless there are moments when the system can't keep up, the battery sits until it's called upon again.

For street cars, a battery should only come into play when you are cranking the engine to start the car, or if you're parked with the engine off listening to the radio or running the cooling fans. An important specification to look for when buying a battery is the number of cold-cranking amps (CCA). This determines the amount of current that the battery can deliver for 30 seconds at 0°F. Most of us aren't worried about how our performance car will crank in these Arctic conditions, but we are concerned about how it will crank after a hot soak on an afternoon cruise. If you have a high-compression, big-cubic-inch engine,

Many choices are available when it comes to a battery and charging system. Things you need to consider are your application and the current draw of the electrical components such as an electric fuel pump, cooling fan(s), air conditioning, stereo, and other electric components.

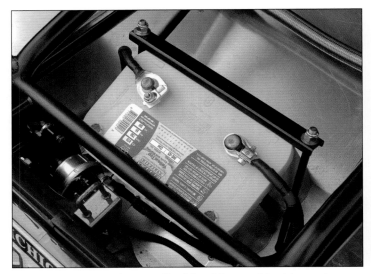

A dry-cell battery has no liquid acid or gel inside and that means it can be mounted in almost any manner you need. In addition, an accident won't cause acid to leak out. Optima offers a variety of dry-cell batteries for performance, racing, and marine use.

Looking for a dry-cell battery but want to keep a restored appearance? TurboStart offers a line of batteries that look original but feature dry-cell technology for a variety of muscle cars.

go with a high-grade battery with 800 or more cold-cranking amps.

Another rating you see on batteries is the reserve capacity. This is the time needed to lower the battery voltage from fully charged to below 10.2 volts with a draw of 25 amps. This is important on racecars that don't use an alternator, as it represents how long a battery delivers voltage above 10.2 volts.

Starting Batteries

These are designed for providing the go-juice for the starter, ignition, and EFI system. These batteries are not designed to go through cycles that nearly drain their charge repeatedly. If you press this kind of cycle activity with a standard battery, its lifetime will be shortened.

Deep-Cycle Batteries

These are designed to handle charging and full discharging over and over again. If you do not run an alternator, you should go with a

deep-cycle battery. However, many of them are not designed to take the brunt of a between-round, high-current mega charge. Most deep-cycle batteries like a longer, low-current charge. It's best to ask the manufacturer to match a battery to your specifications.

Dry-Cell Batteries

For street rods, where mounting the battery can require some creativity, a dry-cell battery is a good idea. Because there's no acid or liquid in these batteries, they can be mounted in any position. Optima, TurboStart, Braille, and XS Power are some of the leading manufacturers in the performance battery market that use absorbed glass mat (AGM) technology in their batteries.

Dual Batteries

Many batteries are available ranging from 12 to 16 and even 18 volts, and racers use them all in different ways. The idea behind a 16-volt bat-

tery is largely extra reserve for racers who do not run an alternator. Benefits do exist for other accessories such as a cooling pump or fan, and the extra voltage can improve output on inductive ignitions.

The most common way to increase capacity in the electrical system is to use dual batteries connected in parallel (positive to positive and negative to negative). In this manner you retain the 12-volt output to run the electrical components on the car, but gain the extra reserve capacity of the extra battery. Two identical batteries should be used if you're running them in parallel. The downside is the weight of having two batteries. You still operate with a 12-volt system, but gain extra capacity with two batteries. I've also heard about some crafty racers connecting two smaller 8-volt tractor-type batteries in series to save weight over dual 12-volt systems.

One thing that racers don't agree on is whether or not they need a

As usual, give racers a little and they want more. This is the case with racing batteries for which 16 volts are desired. The extra reserve is welcome for circle track or drag cars that do not run an alternator. This example is from XS Power. (Photo Courtesy XS Power)

high-voltage battery or dual batteries. Some racers don't even bother with an alternator in drag racing or short-duration circle track events. It all comes down to knowing what your car's electrical system needs to get through a race without falling off in electrical output.

16-Volt Batteries

Batteries that maintain and deliver 16 volts are common in racing applications. TurboStart is well known for its 16-volt battery technology, and they offer a variety of batteries. The main benefit, just as

with running dual batteries, is extra capacity. However, with a 16-volt battery you get the capacity without the added weight. Most 12-volt batteries have a full charge of 12.6 volts, while a TurboStart has 16.8 volts. This extra oomph is achievable with two more cells inside the battery. This is particularly important on race engines that do not incorporate a charging system.

It is interesting to note that stepping up to a 16-volt system does not directly improve the output of a CD ignition control. Most CD ignitions reduce their supply voltage to fit

their needs and let the transformer increase the voltage. That said, a CD ignition's output suffers if the battery voltage begins to drop below 11 volts or so. An inductive ignition, on the other hand (such as the GM HEI), definitely enjoys the benefits of receiving 16 volts.

Remember, an inductive ignition uses the battery voltage to charge the coil; a little more voltage is a good thing with inductive systems. Both systems benefit from the added capacity that a 16-volt battery supplies.

Lithium-Ion Batteries

Exploring the technology behind batteries is never ending, especially in this age of fuel economy and alternate methods of powering automobiles. I'm not going to discuss electric cars, but an emerging battery technology is gaining hold in the performance and racing world: lithium-ion batteries.

Several companies specialize in lithium-ion batteries for performance and racing. Lithium Pros and Braille seem to be leading the charge in the racing world. Lithium-ion is the battery technology for many consumer electronic devices such as cameras and phones or perhaps the electric drill in your toolbox. This is due to their cycling abilities and their constant, slow drains.

Rather than use acid-based cell technology, these batteries use lightweight lithium and carbon, which is a great conductor of heat and electricity as well as being highly reactive.

Typically, this type of battery is considerably higher in price compared to a common lead-based acid battery. Another questionable feature of lithium-ion batteries is that if the battery were to be completely

TurboStart offers several 16-volt batteries. For inductive-based ignition systems such as an HEI distributor, the increased supply voltage can help boost the spark energy. That's not the case with CD-style ignitions. (Photo Courtesy TurboStart)

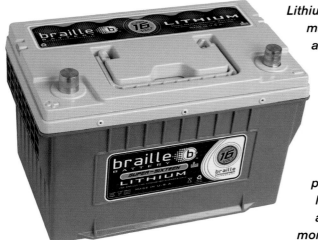

Lithium-ion-based batteries are making their way into racing and with good reason. They weigh a fraction of a typical AGM battery yet still provide incredible output capabilities. Braille Battery has a wide variety of lithium-ion-based batteries for racing and performance. One benefit of lithium-ion batteries is their ability to deep-cycle charge more effectively than any AGM battery. (Photo Courtesy Braille Battery, Inc.)

When you step up to a lithium-ion battery you also need to consider the cost of the corresponding charger. Because lithium-based batteries charge differently than AGM batteries, you need a charger as well. Stick with the same brand of charger as battery. (Photo Courtesy Braille Battery, Inc.)

drained, it would be dead and could not be recharged.

However, these batteries have many positive features. One, especially for racers, is the weight savings and size. A lithium-ion battery can weigh less than half of an equivalent AGM battery without giving up any power or capacity.

In addition, these batteries can handle deep cycling better than traditional batteries and accept a complete charge much quicker. Another benefit that you should consider when shopping for a lithium-ion battery is a built-in battery management system. It monitors the operation of the battery for possible issues such as overheating, excessive current pull, and even low voltage. If the system notices any issues, it can actually disconnect the system from the load. This could save you from draining the battery and being stuck in the middle of nowhere.

Charger

With all of the different battery technologies and materials being used these days, you need to carefully choose the charger. To start with, chargers aren't the bulky, loud humming, heavy machines they used to be. Not that these big ones aren't great to have for heavy-duty shop use, but plenty of modern designs are available.

One point to consider is that most 16-volt batteries require a specific 16-volt charger. Makers of any 16-volt (or more) battery offer a charger recommended for their batteries. If you plan to upgrade to a 16-volt battery supply, plan on the initial expense for a charger as well. This is especially important if you're stepping up to a lithium-ion battery. They absolutely require a different charger.

The latest technology is smart chargers, so-called because of their ability to maintain or bring your battery to full capacity. Most of these chargers are small and designed to be connected while your car sits for long periods of time. The charger constantly monitors the battery condition and knows whether the battery needs to be maintained, charged, or even revived. Another nice feature is that most of these chargers are spark proof and shut off if their leads are reversed on the power and ground side of the battery.

Charging System

Unless you're in a flat-out racecar, you need an alternator to keep the battery charged and provide the voltage and current to the rest of the car. The battery provides the energy to get the car fired up, but once the engine is running, the charging system is responsible for keeping the electrons flowing while maintaining a charge on the battery.

Two types of charging components are used: the generator and the alternator. The voltage regulator is the controller of the system.

Generator

Generators were used on older cars when there wasn't a high demand for current output. A generator is defined as creating a direct current (DC) current, such as an electric motor. The output conductor windings, called the armature, spins inside a stationary magnetic field. The current is induced from the field into the armature, where a direct current is created and used. Generators were limited in their output, especially at

CTEK offers a full line of compact "smart" battery chargers. Many of today's chargers are designed to remain connected when your vehicle sits to maintain the battery and increase its life. Their improved charging process also helps revive very low or sagging batteries.

Large chargers that take up floor space are being downsized into lightweight, easy-to-store models. These relics do still have a place in heavy-duty shop applications.

Between-Round Battery-Charging Tips

Just about every racer puts a charge on the battery between heats or passes down the strip. Here are a few tips and precautions, especially with a 16-volt charger:

- When charging the battery between rounds, always have the system disconnect switch turned off. This prevents other components from being damaged due to the increased voltage of the charger.
- Do not start the car with the charger connected. Once again, the excess voltage could feed through your car's electrical system and damage components.
- Do not try to print out race data information from the car with the charger connected.
- If you have any question about a component's ability to handle 16 volts, contact the manufacturer.

It is common practice for racers who don't use an alternator to charge the battery between rounds. In this case, a deep-cycle battery is a good investment as they're designed for charging and discharging numerous times.

low RPM, at which they were very inefficient.

Alternator

An alternator is really a generator that produces an alternating current (AC) that flows in both directions. The big difference is in its construction: The magnets that produce the magnetic field are connected to the rotor and spin inside the stationary stator assembly. This field is induced into the stator's windings that surround the rotor to achieve a very efficient buildup of current.

The trouble here is that the electrical systems on cars are designed for direct current only. This problem is solved through a series of diodes called a rectifier circuit. It controls the current flow to one useable direction, thus changing it into DC current. This is sometimes referred to as a diode trio and is responsible for changing the AC current to DC for use throughout the car.

Several items must be considered when choosing an alternator, the most important of which is the current draw from the components on your car. The best thing to do is to add up all the electrical components that sap up current. The manufacturer provides most of these specifications.

For example, a typical drag race ignition uses 1 amp per 1,000 rpm, nitrous solenoids can pull up to 15 amps each, water and fuel pumps another 15 or more each, and don't forget all those thumping stereo amps that can put a pretty hefty drain on the system.

Once you have a good idea of the amount of current your car is eating up, you also need to consider the mounting location and the pulley diameter.

Voltage Regulator

Another important part of the alternator and charging circuit is the voltage regulator. It watches over the charging system and determines if more or less output is needed by sensing the voltage in the system. Then it controls the amount that

Remote Mounting and Disconnect Switch

For drag racing, you need an externally operated switch that kills the power through the entire car. If you're racing around in circles, a main kill switch needs to be mounted within reach of the driver. In addition, having one on your street car is not a bad idea as a theft deterrent. Mostly, though, disconnect switches are for racecars.

NHRA mandates that the switch be installed on the main positive wire of the battery and must be capable of shutting off all electrical functions, including the ignition, fuel pumps, fans, etc. The switch must be mounted on the back of the car and the off position must clearly be labeled. If you use a push/pull method, the push motion must shut the system off.

If you have a street car and prefer to keep a stealthy appearance when you're not on the strip, you can install the kill switch inside the trunk, positioned so it toggles forward to turn off and toward the rear to turn on. Then, install a removable steel rod through to the outside of the car that can be pushed to kill the power. When you're not racing, you can remove the rod and no one will be the wiser, except you'll have "push off" written on the back of the car.

On/off switches with a swing handle can be mounted easily. This example is mounted right to the bumper. Also note the easy-to-access battery posts for between-round charging.

Choosing an alternator that meets your car's charging needs is critical. If your car's requirements exceed the output of the charging system, the performance of the ignition, fuel pumps, and other electrical components suffer.

goes into the rotor windings to increase the output and limits output by adding resistance between the battery and the rotor windings. Today, most regulators are inside the alternators, but older cars may have external voltage regulators mounted to the firewall or radiator support.

Pulleys

When you're setting up the alternator for a racecar, the pulley choice is very important. The output of an alternator is dependent on the speed at which it is driven, which is in turn determined by its pulley size. This is important to match to the average RPM that the engine experiences, because an alternator's output is not linear. Its speed makes a big difference in its output.

The alternator to engine pulley ratio is determined by dividing the diameter of the crankshaft pulley by the diameter of the alternator's

The main parts of an alternator include the rotor, stator, diode/rectifier, voltage regulator, and brushes (clockwise from top left). The rotor spins inside the stator assembly to induce a voltage into the stator windings. This creates the AC voltage that is switched to DC voltage through the rectifier. The internal voltage regulator controls the charging rate.

The XS Volt one-wire alternator from Powermaster can be adjusted for use on 12- or 16-volt systems. There is a potentiometer on the back of the housing, so if you move up to a 16-volt system on your racecar, you don't have to change the alternator. (Photo Courtesy Powermaster)

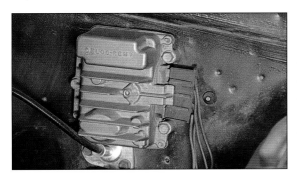

This is an external regulator on a 1965 Pontiac. Since a one-wire alternator with an internal regulator has been installed, the stock regulator is not a part of the charging system anymore. It does help retain the stock appearance of a restored muscle car.

One-Wire Alternator

Many performance alternators available today feature a one-wire connection between the battery and alternator. Some models can be used both ways. The biggest difference is how the alternator turns on. With an OEM-style connection, the alternator is turned on through the ignition switch. One-wire alternators have an internal sensing circuit that wakes up the alternator once it hits a certain RPM. This means that when you start the car, it does not charge until the engine is revved over a certain RPM, generally 1,200 to 1,400 and even more on high-output models. Once the alternator is activated, it charges at low RPM as well.

Installing a one-wire alternator is easy: all you need is one wire between the battery and the alternator. Racing alternators obviously require thicker-gauge wire, and the length of the wire also needs to be taken into consideration. If your car has an external regulator, you need to disconnect it to prevent the dash light indicator from staying on.

Some racers like to switch off the alternator throughout a race, but this is not recommended with one-wire alternators. Severe internal spikes, and damage can be the result of switching it off.

Having only one wire leading to the alternator means less wiring, fewer connections, and fewer chances for problems to arise. It also looks tidier. To activate the charging you need to rev the engine to at least 1,200 rpm.

RECOMMENDED CHARGING CABLE GAUGE SIZE

AMPS	UP TO 4'	4'-7'	4'-7'	4'-7'	4'-7'	4'-7'	4'-7'	4'-7'
35-50	12	12	10	10	10	8	8	8
50-65	10	10	8	8	6	6	6	4
65-85	10	8	8	6	6	4	4	4
85-105	8	8	6	4	4	4	4	2
105-125	6	6	4	4	2	2	2	0
125-150	6	6	4	2	2	2	2	0
150-175	4	4	4	2	2	0	0	0
175-200	2	2	2	2	0	0	0	00

The charge wire between the alternator and the battery is not a place to skimp on size. The length of the wire should determine the gauge size. This chart shows some recommended wire samples. (Photo Courtesy TurboStart)

pulley. Once you know the ratio, you can determine the alternator's RPM by multiplying the ratio by the engine RPM. For example, if you determine the ratio to be 2.1:1, at 2,800 rpm the alternator will be spinning at 5,880 rpm. This sounds like a lot of RPM, but most performance alternators are capable of handling more than 20,000 rpm for short durations, so overdriving the pulley should not present any troubles.

Wiring

Wiring demands patience. Even making a set of plug wires can be time consuming when you take the time to carefully route the wires and add heat guards or accessories. If that pushes the limits of your patience, think about wiring a complete EFI system! After that, you should feel much better about taking your time to ensure that the ignition system is wired correctly.

It is safe to say that half of ignition system problems can be traced to poor wiring, either through cheesy connectors, poor-quality crimps, the wrong style of wiring, or poor wire routing. It can all add up to headaches that may leave you pulling your hair out at the racetrack or, worse yet, on the side of the road.

Choosing a Mounting Position

If you have a new ignition control to install, make a plan. Thinking ahead about where all of the wiring needs to go will save you from hitting roadblocks after you start. Not only will this help when routing the wires to their connections, but it can also help suppress or prevent EMI, which can cause even more headaches.

Most ignition controls are designed to handle underhood con-

Pulley selection is critical to the operation of an alternator. For circle track racing, a good ratio is 1:1 between the engine drive pulley and the alternator pulley. Drag racers want to overdrive the pulley, so 1.75:1 is recommended. Street cars should shoot for about 3:1. Be sure to check out what sizes are available when buying a new alternator.

ditions. If you're not worried about adjusting rev limits or doing anything where you need to access the control, you can choose to put it in an out-of-the-way spot such as under the battery tray. Some ignition controls are potted with an epoxy compound, but some street models are not. If the unit is not potted, do not try to mount it upside down. Doing so would trap any moisture inside, which could present problems down the road.

An ignition control can also be mounted in the interior of your car, such as on the cowling under the dash. Don't put the ignition in an enclosure such as the glove box; having a little air circulation around the area is a good idea, and glove boxes can get warm. If you do install the ignition under the dash, it's imperative to use rubber grommets to route the wires through the firewall. This is especially important with the primary coil wires because they're carrying extremely high voltages.

Connecting the Power Supply Wires

Once a mounting position has been chosen and the box is in place, begin routing the wires to their connectors. The best place for the ignition to be connected is directly to the

battery's positive terminal or from a direct junction off the positive terminal. I've seen these wires connected to the positive side of the starter solenoid, but it really isn't the best place for it because the starter pulls a large amount of current and there are more chances of voltage spikes.

If you're trying to maintain a stock appearance, an ignition control can usually be installed to make it inconspicuous. Here the familiar red MSD 6A box is mounted beneath the battery tray.

Never connect the ignition's power source to the alternator wire. This can cause excessive voltage and current, either of which can damage the ignition control. The best place for the ignition's ground is to the engine block itself, or to the battery's negative terminal.

Once the power supply wires are connected, you can move on to routing the other wires. The coil primary

Vibration mounts are always a good idea to use when mounting the ignition control. Many models are supplied with a set of heavy-duty mounts. Most companies offer them separately for use with other components.

leads are important connections. Remember that these wires can have more than 500 volts pulsing through them. It is best to keep these wires routed separately from the trigger pickup wires to reduce the chance of interference.

When you're deciding on a coil mounting location, keep the high-voltage secondary coil wire shorter than these wires; you don't really want to have to extend these wires. If necessary, use a larger-gauge wire for the extension or even switch the entire wire to an improved thickness. Most 6-Series ignitions use 18-gauge wiring, so stepping up to 16 or even 14 gauge is a good move. Most high-output racing ignitions use 14-gauge wire on their primary leads already.

Routing the Trigger Wires

You should strive to keep the magnetic pickup wires separate from other wiring. These wires carry a voltage signal to tell the ignition when to fire, so you do not want other wiring inducing their voltage

into the trigger wires. These wires should be twisted together to help produce a choke to keep EMI from coming into play. They should be routed separately, and it is best to run them right along the frame or engine for a ground to help isolate their signal.

As more electronics are used in racing applications, such as EFI systems, data acquisition, and retard controls, more chances for interference occur. The best thing you can do to protect the trigger wires is to use a shielded cable that protects the wires through a grounded shield.

Wire Connections

Racecars are taken apart frequently, and that can put quite a strain on the wiring connections. It is important to use high-quality connectors that can be opened and closed hundreds of times and still provide a locked and sealed connection.

Two of the most common connectors used in ignition wiring are Weatherpak connectors, which are mandated on NASCAR ignition harnesses, and Deutsch connectors. Weatherpak connectors have been used for years on OEM applications, and they hold up well. Many accept anywhere from one up to six wires. Each wire has its own seal and barrel, so they cannot short to the terminal next to them. The connectors also lock together, resulting in a sealed and locked connection.

You need a lot of patience when using Weatherpak connectors. You also need an official crimp tool that can crimp the unique terminals correctly. Several versions are available on the market, ranging from high-dollar ones, which do a terrific job, to inexpensive parts-shop models that you should stay away from. MSD

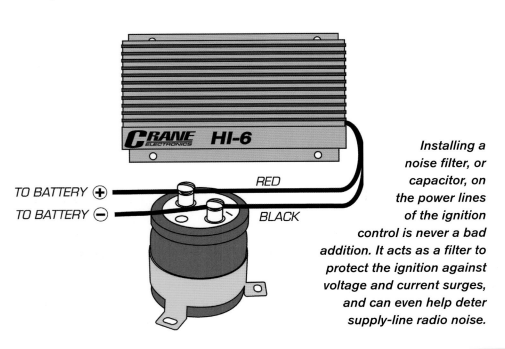

TO BATTERY ⊕

TO BATTERY ⊖

RED

BLACK

Installing a noise filter, or capacitor, on the power lines of the ignition control is never a bad addition. It acts as a filter to protect the ignition against voltage and current surges, and can even help deter supply-line radio noise.

You're Grounded!

Anyone who doesn't take the time to properly ground the ignition system should be the one who gets grounded. Poor electrical grounds can and do result in inconsistencies and erratic performance on racecars and definitely lead to intermittent problems on the street. The ground path is just as important as the positive power source wire, so make sure the ground wiring and paths are up to snuff.

Most racers simply connect the battery ground to the chassis, and then run ground straps from the engine to the chassis. This works, but the best ground path you can create is to run a high-grade copper battery cable straight from the battery negative terminal to the engine block. Even if your battery is mounted in the trunk, the assurance of having this ground is worth the extra work and minor cost of a few more feet of wiring.

Then you can run a heavy-duty wire to the chassis and connect other electrical grounds.

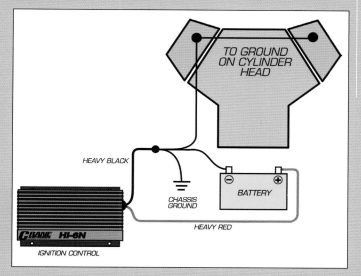

MSD Ignition stresses that when using their Pro-Mag magneto systems ground paths must be routed from both cylinder heads to the common ground for the electrical system. It makes perfect sense when you consider that this is where the voltage jumps from the spark plug electrodes to the ground. If it's required on a high-output system such as a 44-amp magneto, it follows that it's also a good idea to connect your ignition control's ground to the head.

---

offers the Pro-Crimp, which is supplied with crimp dies for spark plug wires. Dies of different styles can be installed in the tool (also available for Deutsch connectors). Once the Weatherpak connectors are assembled, you also need a special tool to remove each terminal in case there's ever a need to repair a wire.

Deutsch connectors are relatively new to the performance aftermarket. MSD has been using them on their Pro Mags for years, and now supplies them on their programmable ignition controls. These connectors have a lot in common with the Weatherpaks; they lock together and are completely sealed. They also require special crimp tools for assembly. One advantage to these connectors is that they can be disassembled without special tools.

Soldering

If you need to make a more permanent connection between wires, such as when adding length, soldering them is the most frequently recommended method. Some debate is still ongoing among wiring pros whether soldering is needed. Many claim that with today's advanced crimp connectors, when properly installed and used, they're as good as a soldered joint. Regardless, twisting wires together does not cut it in the world of performance. It's not even acceptable on a street car.

On racing applications, mounting the coil close to the distributor is always recommended. For street rods or cars that put the coil under the dash, a firewall feed-through is a good idea. These mount to the firewall and provide the added isolation needed to protect the coil wire.

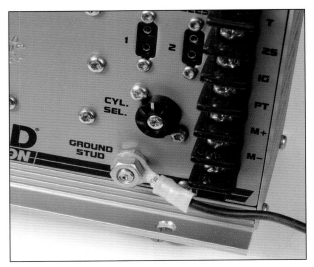

A shielded magnetic pickup cable has a braided piece of wire that surrounds the signal wires. This braided wire gets grounded on one side, generally at the ignition control. This ground effectively shields any voltage noise from other components before they can interfere with the pickup signals. The ignition's ground stud is also useful for other nearby electronics.

Using high-quality, locking, sealed connectors is the only way to go when it comes to ignition components, or any wiring for that matter. Two popular connectors used in ignition wiring are the black Weatherpak connecter and the gray Deutsch connector.

MSD's Pro-Crimp Tool (with replaceable dies) is a ratcheting-style crimp tool that can be used for a variety of crimping jobs. It comes with spark plug wire crimps, but MSD also offers amp-pin jaws, Weatherpak crimp dies, and Deutsch crimp dies.

When you're wiring for performance, you cannot afford a loose connection or, even worse, have it making sporadic connections. Finding a flat-out open or short is much easier than searching for an erratic condition.

Butt-splice connectors are acceptable in certain cases, such as when that section of wire gets moved around, stretched, or pulled; but soldering wires is the best route.

Soldering two wires is the best way to join them together. The connection is solid and acts as an efficient conductor because the solder is an alloy of tin and lead. The one downside is that the connection is a bit brittle, so be sure you know where the wire connection is going to be placed and how it will be used before soldering.

Several different solder materials are available. Most wiring can be handled with a rosin-core material and you can even get it with flux (a kind of the primer) already in the rosin. Aluminum, nickel, and galvanized materials require an acid-core solder.

Relays

A relay is a switching device that lets a small wire with low voltage be used to activate a circuit that requires high voltage and current through a larger-diameter wire. Examples of where a relay is required are with a fuel pump, electric fan, or nitrous solenoid. When these components are initially switched on, there is a larger spike, in addition to the fact that they already pull a lot of current.

MSD offers two relays rated up to 30 amps with an input of 12 volts. The Single-Pole Single-Throw (SPST) model is ideal for single-stage nitrous systems. The Double-Pole

Too Many Connections?

On EFI-equipped cars, a long list of connections needs to be pulled off during an engine swap. Then, when putting the engine back in, all of these wires need to be reconnected. When you're thrashing between rounds, a lot of bad things can happen when an excessive amount of connectors are dealt with. Wiring specialty shops take all of these connectors and wires and route them into one convenient harness and connector.

One example is to route all of the EFI sensor and injector wiring into one big, sealed, locking connector such as the multi-terminal ITT-Cannon connector. The mating connector can then be mounted to the firewall. With that, when the engine has to come out, you only have to pull one connector to do the job! This saves a lot of time and takes the chance of wiring mismatches or breaking important terminal connections out of the picture. This system would probably be useful even on carbureted cars, especially with multiple nitrous systems.

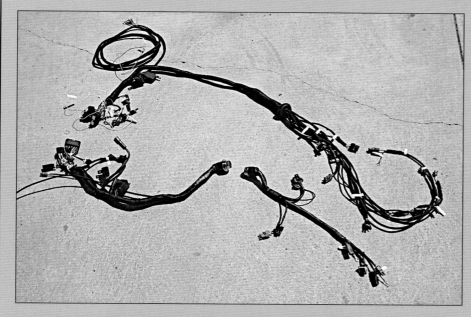

The harness shown on top is the OEM design. The two-part harness on the bottom has been stripped to the needs of a racecar. Note the Cannon Connector in the middle to ease the removal/installation of the engine. The engine side is on the right and the ECU connections are on the left.

This is an ITT-Cannon Connector. When the engine needs to come out, there's only one connector to pull. If you have a multi-engine program, having two harnesses is the way to go.

Testing a CD Ignition Control

The ignition system is generally the first thing that is suspected whenever a race engine hesitates or burbles going down the track. Considering all of the different components that must work in sync to perform correctly, perhaps a little blame is warranted, that is, until the control is proven to be innocent.

I've seen guys in the pits swap out ignition boxes and the coil, only to have the exact same problem. They still come into the pits blaming the ignition. Heads up, racers: If you swap parts and still have the problem, it's time to look somewhere else. Not everyone has spare parts in their trailer, but testers are available that let you simulate running the ignition without taking anything apart.

Mallory, Crane, and MSD offer handy testers that easily connect to the ignition's trigger input wire to make the ignition think the engine is running. These come with a spark plug load tool that you connect to the coil wire and ground. This test plug puts a load on the coil so it has to develop approximately 30,000 volts to jump the gap.

If no spark occurs, connect a different coil and try again. If you now have a spark, the coil is at fault. If there's still no spark, the ignition control may be at fault. Make sure it is properly grounded, that it has battery voltage on the thick red wire, and that 12 volts are on the small red on/off wire.

Another cool thing about this tester is that it has multiple features. Because it has an accurate digital readout of the engine RPM, you can test the accuracy of your tachometer, the shift-light operation, rev limiters, or even RPM-activated switches. Anything that is running off the tach output of the ignition is simulated, which is helpful in setting up rev limits, shift points, and switches.

If you are using a timing accessory such as a retard box, trigger the tester through the control so you can check that it is also working properly. If no spark occurs, bypass the control and trigger the tester through the ignition control. If a spark occurs, the problem has been isolated to the accessory or its wiring.

Check the connections to the trigger source and its output signal wire to the ignition control before assigning blame. Remember, about half the ignition problems that occur are due to poor wiring.

If the ignition and coil check out okay, you need to confirm the operation of your trigger source. This gets a little tougher because there's not much you can check other than resistance on the pickup. Most pickups have proven

An ignition tester saves time, money, and headaches. Hand-held testers send the ignition a trigger signal to trick it into firing just as if the engine were running. You get to control the RPM, and you can even check the RPM limits, switch activation, and the tach. Mallory offers this model. (Photo Courtesy Mallory Ignition)

With the ignition tester connected and the ignition turned off, pull the coil wire off the distributor cap, connect it to the test plug, and clip it to ground. A high-voltage spark is needed to jump the gap so you can tell if the ignition and coil are pulling their weight. It is hot after running the tester, so be careful when removing it.

to be reliable, so check the wiring and connections going to the ignition control.

The other area that needs to be checked is the secondary-side components. Are the rotor tip and cap terminals in good condition? What about the plug wires? Closely check their condition and even check their resistance. Remember, they're not all going to be exact. A bad wire should stand out among the group with very high resistance, or even register an open. Don't forget to check the plugs themselves.

When the ignition checks out okay, it leads to questions about grounds, battery supply, and, of course, the wiring. Once the ignition and electrical systems are cleared of fault, it's time to look into fuel supply and delivery systems, and then on to mechanical components in the engine.

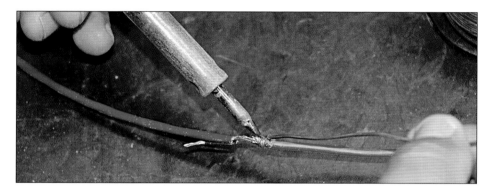

Soldering wire connections is still the best connection you can make between two wires. Always twist the wires together, then apply heat directly to the wires. Once the solder melts (when touched to the wires), let it flow smoothly in and around the wire strands. After the connection cools, seal it with electrical tape or, better yet, shrink-sleeve tubing.

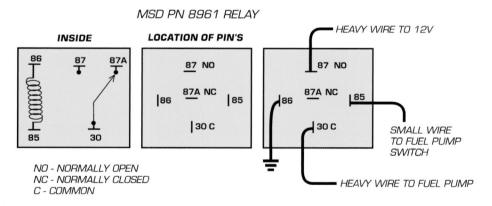

This schematic shows the internal wiring of an SPST relay. For example, when wiring a fuel pump you connect a 14-gauge wire to the fuel pump on terminal 30 and the source wire to the normally open (NO) terminal 87. Ground for the circuit is found on 86, and a small 12-volt on/off wire connects to 85. When the relay is energized through terminals 85 and 86, the armature of the relay is switched over to complete a circuit between 87 and 30 to feed the high current to the fuel pump.

Double-Throw (DPDT) model can supply high voltage and current to two components.

Relays have two separate circuits internally. One is the switch, and the other acts as the controller. When the controller side is energized through the low-current side, it creates a magnetic field inside the relay that controls the switching side. The switching side activates or deactivates a high-current circuit through a normally open (NO) or normally closed (NC) switch.

Relays have many uses, from horns to headlights to air shifter solenoids. Once you wire one and see how nice they function, you'll be hooked.

When you're wiring your ignition or any circuit in your car, it is always a good idea to take notes as to where a circuit is connected and with what color wires. This is especially true when relays and other switches are involved. Like mapping out a plan for installing ignition parts, knowing how your relays are installed and when they're supposed to be functioning will help you in times of repair or troubleshooting.

Definitions and Diagrams
Useful Info and Wiring Schematics

By now you should have a much better grasp of what you need to make your car fire up. As you search through catalogs, websites, and ads, you notice output numbers and specifications given for just about anything used in an ignition system. Unfortunately, those sources don't include explanations of each measurement; the following list should be a helpful way to wrap up the discussion about performance ignitions.

Current: This refers to the flow of electrons through a conductor. It is measured in amps (I).

Ohm's Law: This is a formula that helps figure out an unknown in an electrical circuit when two of the three are known. It states that amperage varies in a direct ratio to voltage (amperage increases as voltage increases), while it is inversely proportional to resistance (amperage decreases as resistance increases). The formula is: $E = I \times R$, where E is electrical voltage, I is current, and R is resistance.

Operating Voltage: This is the amount of voltage that the ignition control or device requires to operate at its full potential. Most ignition controls are designed to operate at full output with 10 to 18 volts. Once the voltage dips below 10 volts, the engine keeps running, but the ignition is not operating at its full potential and engine performance begins to decline. This is why it is so important to have a fully charged battery in cases when a charging system is not used.

Operating Current: The current or amperage that a CD ignition control draws is extremely important. As engine RPM increases, the ignition draws more current from the battery in order to produce more output. The thing to keep in mind here is that you may have a lot of other circuits pulling current from the battery as well. Water pumps, fuel pumps, nitrous solenoids, electric fans, and other accessories use current, and they also generally increase their draw as RPM increases. Be sure to have a charging system or battery that can meet the current demands of your system. For inductive ignition systems, this refers to the maximum amount of current that is going into the coil.

Output Voltage: This specification, also called secondary voltage, is a measure of how much voltage is produced through the secondary windings of the coil. This is the most common specification used to judge coils, and perhaps the most misinterpreted as well. When you see a coil rated at 50,000 volts, it is referring to its output potential. It could handle that amount of voltage, although in the real world it will probably never see 50,000 volts. Remember, an ignition only uses as much voltage as it needs to jump the plug gap, and rarely does that ever require 50,000 volts. The secondary side of the ignition really isn't able to handle that amount of voltage.

Numerous variables determine output voltage: ignition type, the coil turns ratio, the energy of the ignition, the construction of the coil, and more. It is important to have a good-quality coil that is capable of delivering high voltage when it needs to.

Resistance: Resistance is opposition to the flow of current, and is measured in ohms.

Spark Energy: This is a measure of how much "heat" is produced at the spark plug gap. It is a product of voltage, current, and time. It is measured in joules or millijoules in most ignition cases. Inductive ignitions use this to indicate the amount of energy that is stored in the coil.

Spark Duration: This is how long the spark burns in the cylinder. Some companies list this as the amount of time that the multiple sparks occur. Most multiple-sparking ignitions provide a spark series that lasts for 20 degrees of crankshaft rotation. When this spec is mentioned in association with coils, it refers to a single spark and is measured in microseconds.

Voltage: This is an electrical force that causes current to flow through a circuit or conductor. Its specification is given in volts (E). Confusion arises occasionally because the symbol for magnetic voltage is V.

Troubleshooting Your CD Ignition

An ignition tester is a great tool, but not everyone has one in his or her toolbox (although it is highly recommended for racers). The operation of your CD ignition control and coil can be checked by other methods just to make sure they're doing their job.

This test is generally more helpful on no-start conditions, as you aren't able to run any RPM; with 10 or 20 rpm you can confirm that a spark occurs.

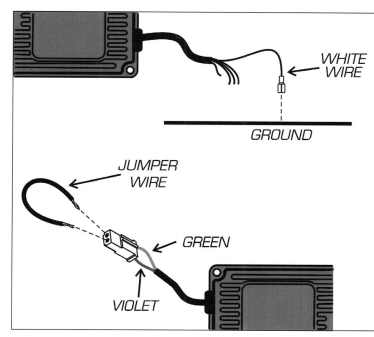

These diagrams illustrate how to check for spark on most CD ignition controls. Remove the coil wire and place it close to ground. Turn the key to on and tap the white wire to ground (or jump the mag pickup terminals together) rapidly. A spark should jump to ground. If no spark occurs, try another coil.

With the ignition off, remove the coil wire from the distributor cap. Position it within 1/2 inch from a ground. Next, disconnect the trigger source from the distributor or crank trigger pickup. Now, turn the ignition on, but don't crank the engine.

If you are using the single-wire input of the ignition control, tap it to ground several times quickly. You are the substitute for the trigger signal. Every time the wire is removed from ground, a spark should jump from the coil wire to ground. If you are using a magnetic pickup, connect the two wires with a paper clip or piece of wire, and then break the connection. A spark should jump from the coil wire to ground.

When the ignition checks out okay, it leads to questions about the distributor pickup, grounds, battery supply, and of course, the wiring. Once the ignition and electrical systems are cleared of fault, it's time to look into fuel supply and delivery systems, and then on to mechanical components in the engine.

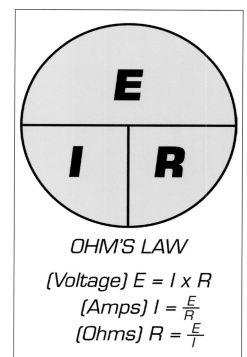

OHM'S LAW

(Voltage) $E = I \times R$

(Amps) $I = \frac{E}{R}$

(Ohms) $R = \frac{E}{I}$

This is the infamous pie chart that illustrates Ohm's Law. You can figure out the voltage, current, or resistance of a circuit by plugging in two values. This can be handy when building different circuits or figuring out voltage and current requirements.

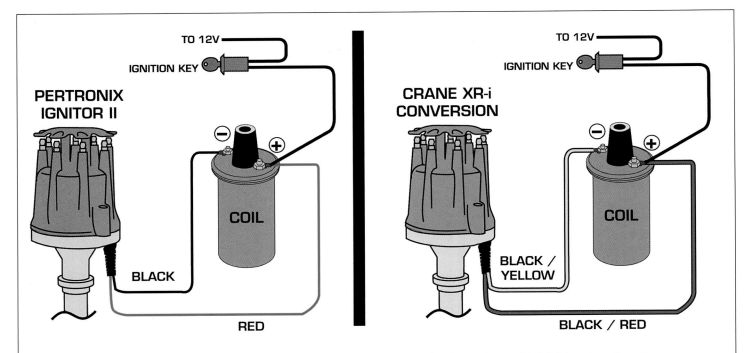

TO 12V
IGNITION KEY

**PERTRONIX
IGNITOR II**

COIL

BLACK

RED

TO 12V
IGNITION KEY

**CRANE XR-i
CONVERSION**

COIL

BLACK /
YELLOW

BLACK / RED

These diagrams show the wiring of two-point replacement kits, Pertronix (left) and Crane (right). They install easily into your stock distributor in place of the breaker points, making adjustments and wear a thing of the past. The only sign that electronics are inside the distributor are the two wires coming out. Because these kits are electronic, they require a 12-volt source.

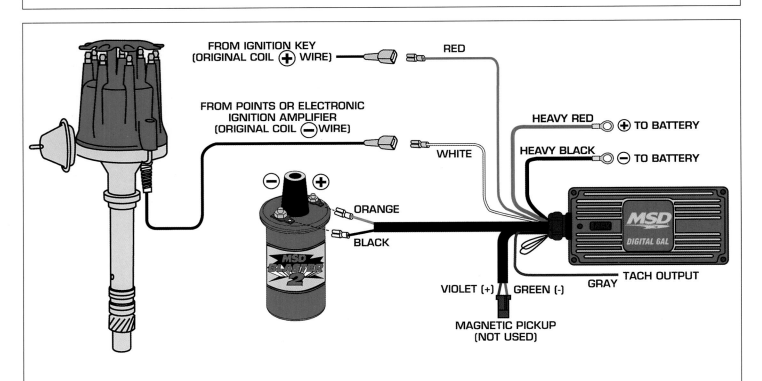

FROM IGNITION KEY
(ORIGINAL COIL + WIRE)

RED

FROM POINTS OR ELECTRONIC
IGNITION AMPLIFIER
(ORIGINAL COIL — WIRE)

WHITE

HEAVY RED — + TO BATTERY

HEAVY BLACK — — TO BATTERY

ORANGE

BLACK

MSD
DIGITAL 6AL

TACH OUTPUT

GRAY

VIOLET (+)   GREEN (-)

MAGNETIC PICKUP
(NOT USED)

If your points distributor is in good working condition and you don't plan to rev the engine through racing-type RPM, you can run an ignition control with the stock points. The points last longer because they're operating merely as a switching device, plus you get the benefits of the CD sparks from the ignition.

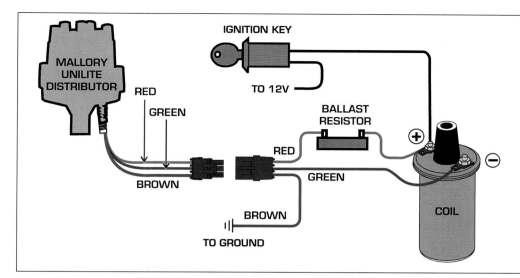

The Mallory Unilite distributor is a popular alternative to distributors with breaker points. The electronic distributor uses a maintenance-free optical sensor to trigger the ignition. It is easy to install with only three wires to connect, plus its small housing fits in tighter areas that an HEI or even a standard-size housing. This makes them ideal for street rods.

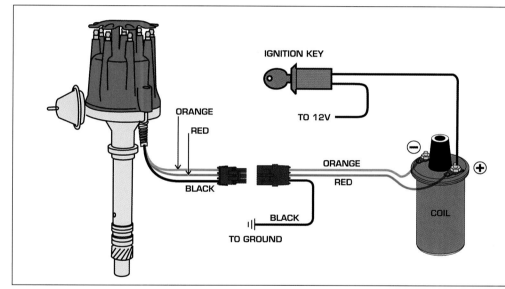

The MSD Ready-to-Run Distributor is a self-contained electronic distributor. Its electronic module is triggered by a magnetic pickup. The module is an inductive ignition design that connects to the coil's negative and positive terminals and a ground wire.

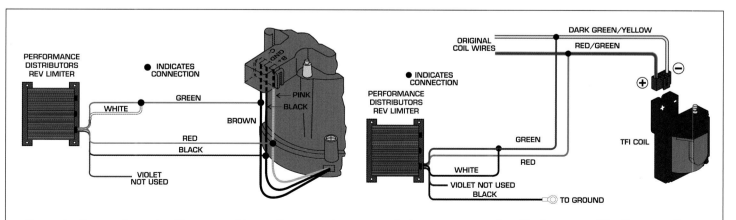

If you don't run a fancy ignition control but still want to have a rev limiter on your engine, Performance Distributors offers a rev control that operates with factory inductive ignition systems. The control is easy to install and the RPM limits are adjusted with popular plug-in modules.

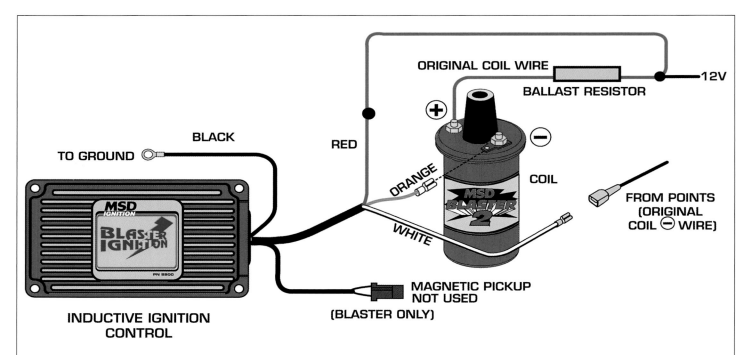

If you're looking for a little more oomph from your engine while staying within a budget, several inductive ignitions are available that fit the bill. Most of these controls put a little more current to the coil while improving the dwell control of the ignition. Installation is simple, with only a trigger source, 12-volt input, and a coil negative connection.

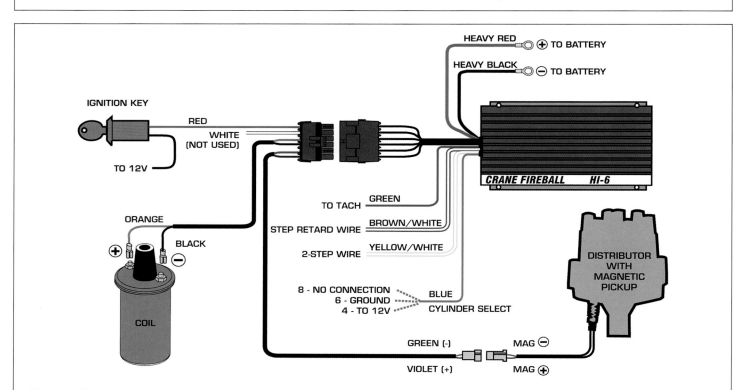

Most multiple-sparking capacitive discharge ignitions install the same way. It is important to note that the only wires that connect to the coil primary terminals come from the ignition. Never connect a test light, tach, or other accessory to coil terminals with a CD ignition. This diagram shows a Fireball HI-6 wired to a distributor with a magnetic pickup.

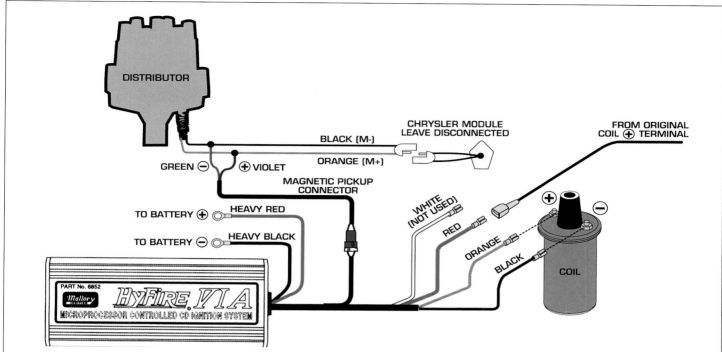

Because Chrysler used a magnetic pickup in its distributors, the ignition's magnetic pickup input wires can be spliced to the distributor. It is important to disconnect the factory harness from the stock ignition module. A Chrysler electronic ignition can also use the points/amplifier (white wire) input. Going from the distributor pickup bypasses the ignition module completely (as shown).

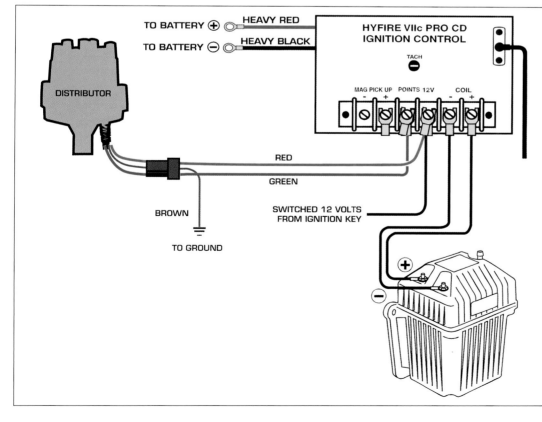

If you already have a Mallory Unilite distributor but want to upgrade to one of their CD ignition controls, you don't need a new distributor. The Unilite can be easily wired to provide a trigger input signal to the ignition controls. The green wire is the trigger source and simply needs to be connected to the points or magnetic positive terminal of the ignition.

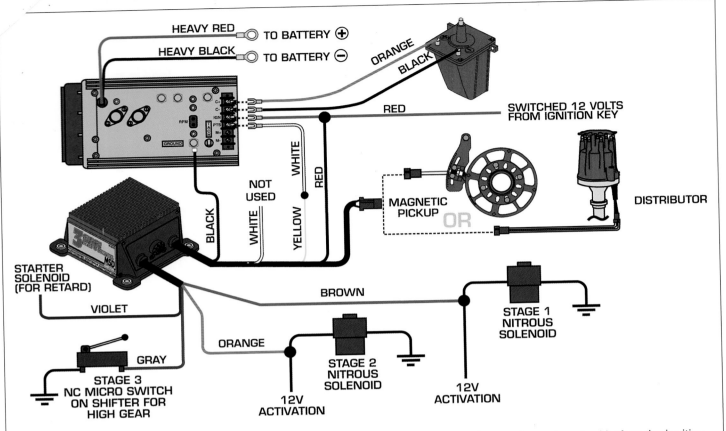

Adding a timing accessory control box is easy. Just remember that the timing control must always be wired before the ignition. Two inputs are on the timing accessory for points/amplifier or magnetic pickup, as on the ignition control. An output connects to the ignition's points/amplifier input wire. This diagram shows a complete multi-step retard wiring on an MSD 7AL-2 system.

The Electromotive XDI ignition is a whole different ball game with its dual-output coils and conspicuously absent distributor. However, the ignition is almost too easy to wire and install. This diagram shows the installation with a relay, so there is no draw when the key is off. The relay isn't necessary in all installations.

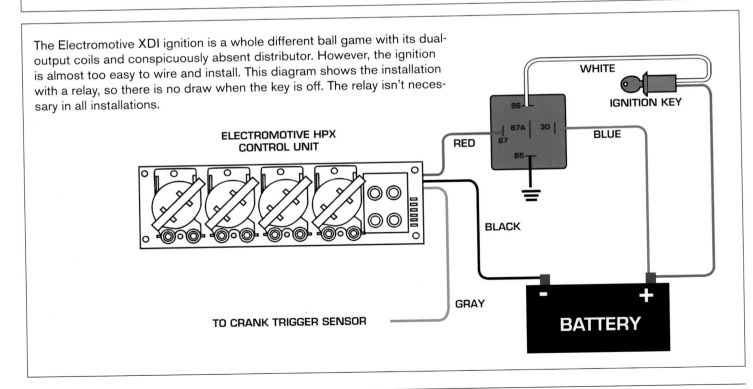

Wiring an Ignition Control to an HEI

Even though they haven't been offered on a new car in nearly two decades, the GM HEI is one of the most popular distributors available. Many new crate engines are supplied with a brand-new HEI distributor, and most ignition companies offer accessories and even complete HEI distributors.

General Motors produced a couple different versions of the HEI. When you're upgrading your ignition, you need to know which model you are using in order to complete the installation correctly. The difference between the models has to do with the number of terminals that the ignition module has: four, five, or seven.

The four-pin version has a vac-uum advance canister and is the most popular. The five- and seven-pin models came on later-model vehicles and incorporated a knock sensor or some sort of electronic timing control.

Installations vary by using the magnetic pickup of the ignition or its points/amplifier input. The HEI module may be used or removed from the housing.

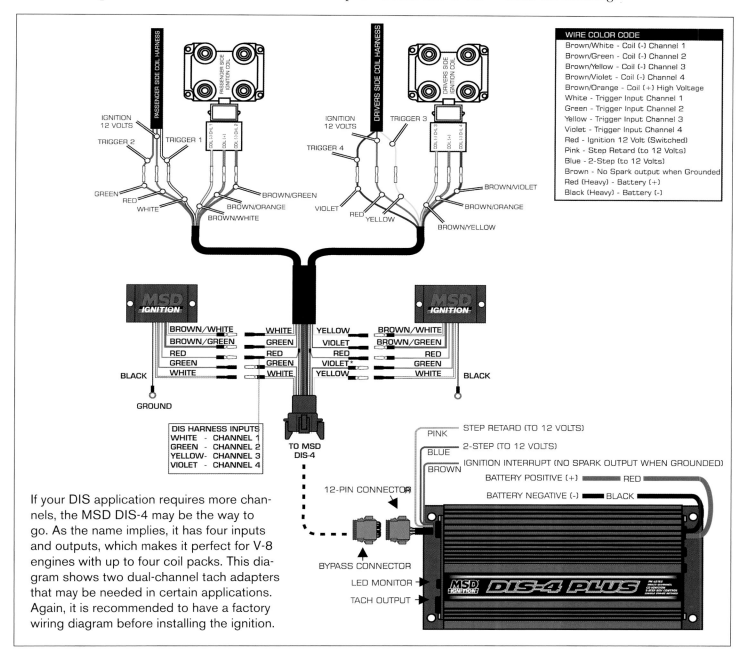

If your DIS application requires more channels, the MSD DIS-4 may be the way to go. As the name implies, it has four inputs and outputs, which makes it perfect for V-8 engines with up to four coil packs. This diagram shows two dual-channel tach adapters that may be needed in certain applications. Again, it is recommended to have a factory wiring diagram before installing the ignition.

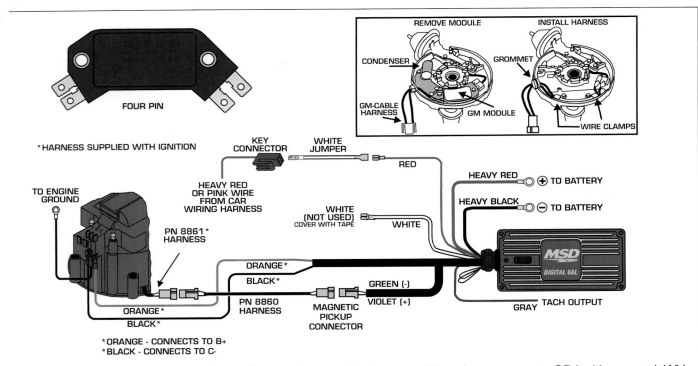

When you have a four-pin HEI module (top left), it must be completely removed in order to connect a CD ignition control. With the module removed, a small harness is connected to the trigger pickup and routed to the ignition's magnetic pickup connector. Notice that the white wire of the ignition control is not used.

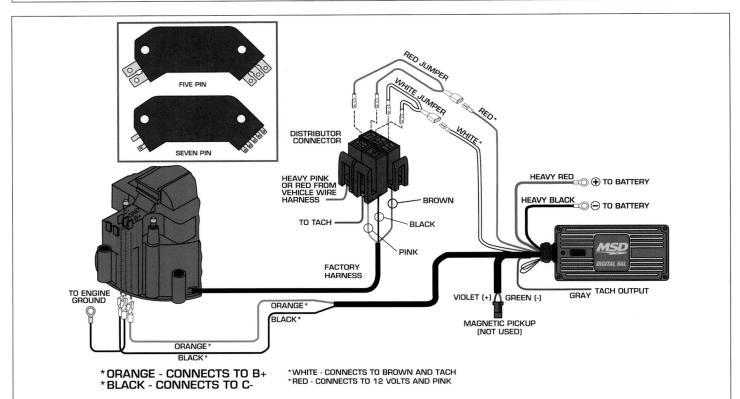

An HEI that uses a five- or seven-pin module uses the single white wire trigger for points or amplifiers, rather than the magnetic pickup. These distributors can be identified by their lack of a vacuum advance canister, although some five-pin models retain the canister. For these installations, the module stays in the distributor and the trigger signal comes through the module.

The Power Grid is the next evolution in MSD's programmable ignition controls. The programming part of the ignition has been separated from the ignition so it can be used with different systems such as an MSD-8 or Pro-Mag. This diagram shows it connecting to its sibling ignition control.

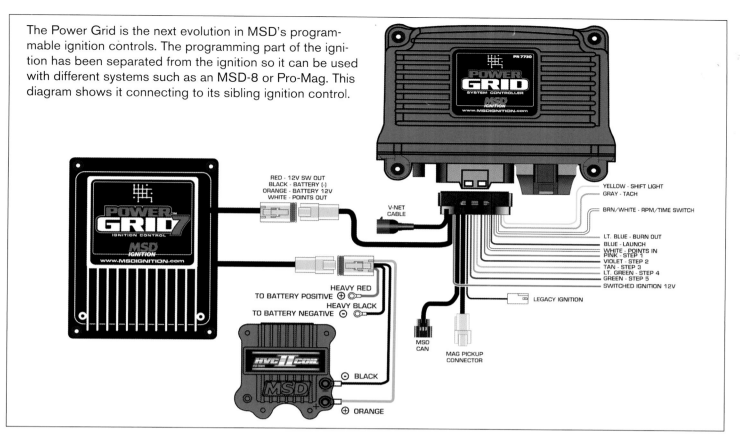

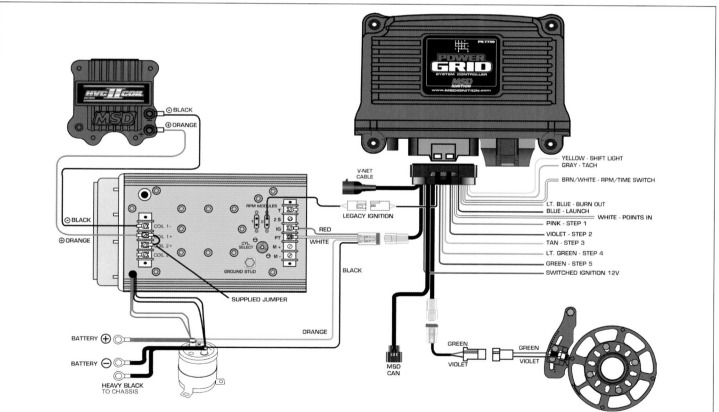

The Power Grid can easily control the thunderous spark of the MSD-8 Plus Ignition Control. As with any application where timing and RPM are being manipulated, a crank trigger is highly recommended to trigger the ignition. The crank trigger signal is input into the Power Grid. It manipulates the signal and sends to the PTS (points) input of the MSD-8 to fire the coil.

SOURCE GUIDE

Accel
10601 Memphis Ave., #12
Cleveland, OH 44144
216-658-6413
www.accel-ignition.com

Autolite
800-890-2075
www.autolite.com

Braille
6935 15th St. E., Bldg. 115
Sarasota, FL 34243
941-312-5047
www.braillebattery.com

Compu-Tronix
20470 Carrey Rd.
Walnut, CA 31789
909-598-0220
www.compu-tronix.com

Crane Cams
1830 Holsonback Dr.
Daytona Beach, FL 32117
386-310-4875
www.cranecams.com

Denso
3900 Via Oro Ave.
Long Beach, CA 90810
310-834-6352
www.globaldenso.com

Electromotive Inc.
9131 Centreville Rd.
Manassas, VA 20110
703-331-0100
www.electromotive-inc.com

Jesel
1985 Cedarbridge Ave., Ste. A
Lakewood, NJ 08701
732-901-1800
www.jesel.com

Lithium Pros
4123 Topeka St.
Knoxville, TN 37917
865-688-2083
www.lithiumpros.com

Mallory
10601 Memphis Ave., No. 12
Cleveland, OH 44144
216-658-6413
www.mallory-ignition.com

Moroso
80 Carter Dr.
Guilford, CT 06437-0570
203-453-6571
www.moroso.com

MSD Performance
1490 Henry Brennan Dr.
El Paso, TX 79936
915-857-5200
www.msdperformance.com

Optima Batteries
5757 N. Green Bay Ave.
Milwaukee, WI 53209
888-867-8462
www.optimabatteries.com

Performance Distributors
2699 Barris Dr.
Memphis, TN 38123
901-396-5782
www.performancedistributors.com

Pertronix
440 East Arrow Hwy.
San Dimas, CA 91773
909-599-5955
www.pertronix.com

Powerhouse Products
3402 Democrat Rd.
Memphis, TN 38118
901-795-7600
www.powerhouseproducts.com

Powermaster Performance
1833 Downs Dr.
West Chicago, IL 60185
630-849-7754
www.powermastermotorsports.com

TurboStart/Axion Power
    International
3601 Clover Ln.
New Castle, PA 16105
724-654-9300
www.turbostart.com

XS Power
2847 John Deere Dr., No. 102
Knoxville, TN, 37917
865-688-5953
www.4xspower.com